THE HUMAN INTERFACE

ADAPTING TO LIFE WITH AI

THE ALGORITHMIC MIND
BOOK 3

GARI JOHNSON

GTM APAC

The Human Interface: Adapting to Life with AI Book 3 of The Algorithmic Mind Series

Published by Gari Johnson Books, Sydney, Australia.

Second edition, 2026. First published 2025.

Series Information:

The Algorithmic Mind is a three-book series that examines the impact of artificial intelligence on society and human agency.

- Book 1: The Mirror Problem, How AI Reflects Our Worst Selves
- Book 2: The Surveillance Mirror, How AI Shapes Human Behaviour
- Book 3: The Human Interface, Adapting to Life with AI

Cover and interior design by the Author

Disclaimer:

The views and opinions expressed in this book are those of the author and do not necessarily reflect the official policy or position of any organisation, employer, or institution with which the author has been affiliated. The information provided is for educational and informational purposes only.

This book contains both real examples and composite illustrations. Composite voices are drawn from documented patterns rather than specific individuals; they are identifiable by the absence of footnote cues. Any voice without a superscript note is a composite. Where real research, companies, or events are referenced, proper citations are provided.

Contact Information: For speaking engagements, media enquiries, or bulk sales, please contact the author. Email: gari.johnson@icloud.com Website: www.gtmapac.com

Publisher's Note: This book contains references to real companies, products, and services for illustrative purposes. All trademarks and trade names are the property of their respective owners and are used here for identification purposes only.

Formatted with Vellum

THE TURING TEST IN REVERSE

Alan Turing proposed a test for machine intelligence. Could a computer convince a human that it was human? He did not anticipate the version of the world we now live in: humans trying to convince algorithms that we are worth their attention. We write our CVs for applicant tracking systems, the automated software that screens applications before any human recruiter sees them, tune our social media posts for engagement algorithms, and speak to voice assistants like they are slightly dense but well-meaning flatmates who happen to control the heating.

If you have ever found yourself saying 'please' and 'thank you' to Alexa (and feeling oddly guilty when you do not), or carefully curating your LinkedIn posts to appease the mysterious engagement gods, or explaining your lifelong passion for customer service in a cover letter that you know will be read by a machine, congratulations, you have failed the reverse Turing test. You are acting more like a machine than the machines are.

This third volume in The Algorithmic Mind series explores what happens when artificial intelligence ceases to be artificial and becomes intimate. Not in the sci-fi sense of robot romance (though there is a concerning amount of that too), but in the mundane, everyday sense of living with systems that know us better than we know ourselves and shape our behaviour in ways we are only beginning to understand.

This is the third and final volume in the series, and it closes a sequence. Book 1 examined how AI reflects our biases at us. Book 2 examined how it shapes our behaviour. This one examines how we are adapting to live with it, and how that adaptation is changing what it means to be human. From teenagers who have never known life without algorithmic recommendations to middle-aged professionals having existential crises about their relevance in an automated world, we are all becoming interfaces in the human-AI system.

A NOTE ABOUT THIS BOOK

This book contains both real examples and composite illustrations. The composite voices you will meet, people such as Sarah managing career transitions or Marcus discovering algorithmic dating biases, represent documented patterns drawn from research and interviews. You can identify composite voices by the absence of footnote cues: any named person without a superscript note is a composite figure. Where real research, companies, or events are referenced, citations are provided, and footnote cues are used. This approach is consistent across all three volumes in the series.

In writing this book, I used artificial intelligence tools, including Claude for research assistance and content development, and Grammarly for editing support. There is an obvious joke in writing a book about human-AI collaboration with the help of an AI, and I have decided to leave it where it lies.

This is the second edition, reflecting the state of play as of mid-2026; the first edition's errors have been corrected based on the best evidence I could find. No technical background is assumed. If you have ever said please to a voice assistant, you are the intended reader.

The title, 'The Human Interface,' borrows the technical term for how humans interact with computers and turns it on its head. Here, the human is the interface: the layer that translates between the algorithmic world and the messy, unpredictable business of human experience. We translate between human needs and algorithmic capabilities, mediate between emotional intelligence and the artificial kind, and serve as unpaid customer service representatives for systems we did not design and cannot fully control.

This is not a book about the singularity or superintelligence. Those conversations have their place, and they tend to skip past the more immediate reality. We already live in a world shaped by artificial intelligence, and most of it is profoundly ordinary. Your phone's autocorrect knows your typing patterns better than your closest friend knows your voice. Your streaming service has stronger opinions about tonight's viewing than you do. Your smart thermostat has learned your schedule and started making comfort decisions you never authorised.

The challenge is not preparing for a distant future in which machines take over. It is holding on to human agency and dignity in a present where machines already make thousands of micro-decisions about our lives every day. The intelligence in question is less 'artificial general intelligence' and more 'artificial middle management': bureaucratic, occasionally helpful, often inexplicable, and surprisingly influential over how the day goes.

As you will discover in the pages that follow, this challenge manifests differently across generations, industries, and cultures. A 16-year-old who grew up with TikTok's algorithm curating their worldview has a fundamentally different relationship with AI than a 50-year-old manager trying to understand why their team is suddenly obsessed with 'prompt engineering.' A tech company that uses sophisticated AI to optimise everything except its own productivity presents a different puzzle than a government trying to regulate systems that evolve faster than legislative processes.

The humour in this book serves the same purpose as in the previous volumes. It is a way of maintaining critical distance from systems that can feel overwhelmingly complex or intimidatingly powerful. When we can laugh at the absurdity of having to explain to our cars that we really do want to take this particular route home, despite what the GPS thinks, we are asserting a form of human agency that pure technical analysis might miss.

The interface between humans and AI is technological, psychological, social, cultural, and political. How we adapt to these systems, and how they change us as we do so, is harder to predict than their next capability, and it matters more to daily life. The question that runs through this book is less about what the machines will be able to do and more about what kind of humans we will become once we are living with them.

Welcome to the interface. Mind the gap between the human and the artificial. It is wider than it appears, and stranger than anyone expected.

PART I

LIFE STAGES IN THE AGE OF ALGORITHMS

1

THE AI MID-LIFE CRISIS

WHEN YOUR SMART HOME IS SMARTER THAN YOUR CAREER PLAN

There is a particular moment in modern middle age when you realise that your TikTok algorithm understands you better than your performance review ever has. It is usually around 2 AM, when you are scrolling through videos that somehow perfectly capture your existential dread about career relevance, financial insecurity, and the creeping suspicion that the skills you have spent decades developing might be as obsolete as your university's computer lab.

The AI midlife crisis is a uniquely 21st-century phenomenon affecting the sandwich generation caught between ageing parents who need help turning on their tablets and children who assume artificial intelligence is as natural as gravity. These are the 40-somethings who built their careers on expertise that is being automated, who have saved for retirement in pension funds that invest in the very companies making them redundant, and who find themselves explaining decades of experience to recruitment systems that think 'Python' refers exclusively to programming languages rather than, say, Monty Python.

The traditional midlife crisis typically involves buying a sports car and reevaluating life choices. The AI midlife crisis involves your smart home thermostat making better scheduling decisions than you do. At the same time, you wonder whether 'prompt engineer' is a real job title or an elaborate millennial prank.

THE NHS ALGORITHM PARADOX

Rachel, an emergency medicine doctor with fifteen years' experience at a Greater Manchester NHS trust, discovered the paradox firsthand. She can diagnose pneumonia from the way a patient breathes, spot depression in the tilt of someone's shoulders, and manage complex family dynamics around end-of-life care with a wisdom that comes only from experience. When the NHS introduced AI diagnostic-assistance tools in her practice, she found herself in a peculiar position, arguing with a computer about whether her patient actually had the symptoms the algorithm insisted they had.

'The system kept flagging a perfectly healthy 34-year-old for heart disease risk because his postcode suggested higher stress levels, his Fitbit showed irregular sleep patterns, and his shopping history included too many ready meals,' Rachel explains. 'I've examined him. He's fine. But the algorithm was so confident in its assessment that the hospital administration suggested I might be missing something.'

She ordered the tests. They revealed a rare congenital heart condition that could have caused sudden death if undiagnosed. The AI had potentially saved a life, but Rachel felt profoundly unsettled by the experience. 'I've spent fifteen years learning to read patients,' she explains. 'Now I'm learning to read machines that read patients. It's medicine, but it's not medicine as I know it.'[1]

Rachel's colleague, David, a 52-year-old radiologist who initially resisted the AI systems, has become one of their strongest advocates, not because the technology replaced his expertise, but because it freed him to focus on what he does best: interpreting complex cases, communicating with patients, and mentoring younger doctors.

'The AI handles the routine scans: the obvious fractures, the clear pneumonias,' David explains. 'That gives me time for the difficult cases, the ones that need human judgment. I'm actually using my expertise more, not less. The crisis wasn't about being replaced; it was about learning to collaborate with something that thinks differently than I do.'

(Healthcare AI is examined in depth in Chapter 5, which is where it belongs. What Rachel and David illustrate here is the broader psychological transition that faces anyone whose expertise was built before algorithms joined the room.)

THE ABSURDITY OF RETRAINING ADVICE CYCLES

If you have reached your 40s in the 21st century, you have lived through at least three rounds of well-meaning career advice that promised to future-proof your professional life. First, it was 'learn to code.' Computer programming would secure your place in the digital economy. Then it was 'learn to prompt.' The ability to communicate effectively with AI systems would become the new essential skill. Now, increasingly, it is 'learn to cope', accepting that technological obsolescence is inevitable and focusing on developing emotional resilience.

This cycle reveals something about how we misunderstand technological change. Each wave of advice assumes that the solution to technological disruption is more technology. That if you can just master the right digital skill, you will be safe from the next wave of automation.

Consider Sarah, a 47-year-old marketing manager in Birmingham who dutifully learned Python programming when digital transformation hit her industry, then retrained in data analytics as machine learning became essential, and finally took courses in prompt engineering as generative AI emerged. Each time, she was told she was investing in her future. Each time, the future evolved faster than her ability to keep up with it.

'Every course promised the same thing,' Sarah says. 'Invest now, stay relevant. But the ground kept moving. Each new skill was out of date before I'd had a chance to use it properly.'[2]

Yet not everyone shares Sarah's experience. Tomoko, a 48-year-old supply chain manager in Tokyo, successfully pivoted her career by focusing not on specific technical skills but on the human elements that AI struggles to replicate. 'I stopped trying to compete with the machines on data processing,' she explains. 'Instead, I became the person who could explain AI decisions to sceptical stakeholders, negotiate with suppliers who didn't trust algorithmic pricing, and manage the human anxiety that comes with automation.'[3]

Tomoko's success suggests that the real tragedy is not that specific skills become obsolete. It is the constant retraining cycle that prevents people from developing the deeper capabilities that might actually provide resilience: critical thinking, emotional intelligence, systems thinking, and the kind of wisdom that comes from decades of experience working within complex human organisations.

WHEN TEENAGERS' TIKTOK ALGORITHMS UNDERSTAND YOU BETTER THAN YOUR BOSS

Nothing illustrates the AI midlife crisis more perfectly than the moment when you realise that your 16-year-old's social media algorithm has a more sophisticated understanding of human psychology than your workplace's 'data-driven' management system.

TikTok's recommendation engine can detect subtle mood shifts, predict which content will resonate with different emotional states, and adjust its approach based on the time of day, recent viewing patterns, and contextual cues that most humans would miss. It understands that the same person might want inspirational content in the morning, educational videos during lunch breaks, and absurdist comedy at 11 PM.

Meanwhile, at work, the performance management system still assumes that all employees are motivated by the same metrics, that productivity can be measured uniformly across different roles, and that annual reviews provide meaningful insights into professional development needs.

Michael, a 45-year-old financial analyst in London, describes the disconnect: 'My daughter's TikTok knows she's stressed about exams before she does. It starts showing her calming content and study tips. But my company's AI performance system gave me a low engagement score because I didn't attend enough virtual happy hours during lockdown. The consumer AI understands human complexity; the enterprise AI treats us like spreadsheet entries.'

This comparison is not entirely fair. TikTok has access to vastly more data points and can experiment with millions of users simultaneously, while workplace systems face legal and ethical constraints that social media platforms largely ignore. But the contrast illuminates something important about how algorithmic intelligence develops.

EXPLAINING DECADES OF EXPERIENCE TO AI RECRUITMENT SYSTEMS

One of the most surreal aspects of the modern job search is the realisation that your primary audience is not a human recruiter who might appreciate nuance, context, and the storytelling that makes a career trajectory meaningful. It is an applicant tracking system that processes your professional history like a shopping list.

According to research by Harvard Business School and Accenture, 88% of employers surveyed acknowledged rejecting qualified high-skilled candidates through automated screening, and 94% said the same for middle-skilled candidates: the systems designed to reduce bias were, in many cases, eliminating qualified candidates before any human eye ever saw their application.[4]

Consider Marcus, a 52-year-old former newspaper editor in Cape Town transitioning to corporate communications. His CV tells a rich story of adapting to technological change, from typesetting to desktop publishing, from print-only to multimedia storytelling, from traditional journalism to data-driven content strategy. He has managed teams through industry upheaval, developed crisis communication strategies for rapidly changing news environments, and built expertise in audience analysis that predates but anticipates social media marketing.

To a human recruiter, this background suggests adaptability, leadership under pressure, and a deep understanding of how communication strategies must evolve in response to technological change. To an applicant tracking system scanning for specific software proficiencies and job titles, it is a CV that does not match current requirements because it lacks sufficient instances of terms such as 'SEO optimisation,' 'growth hacking,' or 'conversion funnel management.'

But Marcus found a way through. Working with a career coach who understood both human psychology and ATS algorithms, he learned to create what she called 'bilingual CVs', documents that speak to both machines and humans. 'You have to reverse-engineer your story,' the coach explained. 'Start with what the algorithm needs to see, then layer in the human narrative. It's like writing poetry that also functions as a technical manual.'

THE PSYCHOLOGICAL IMPACT AND PATH FORWARD

The psychological dimension of the AI mid-life crisis extends far beyond career concerns into fundamental questions of identity, purpose, and social value. For many professionals in their 40s and 50s, the timing is particularly cruel. They are reaching the peak of their expertise just as that expertise becomes potentially obsolete, facing their highest financial obligations just as their earning potential becomes uncertain.

Dr Tanaka, a psychologist studying technology-related career anxiety in Osaka, describes this as 'expertise vertigo', the disorienting experience of having deep knowledge become suddenly shallow. 'These are people who spent decades becoming experts in their fields,' she explains. 'They understand complex systems, have developed sophisticated judgment, and can manage ambiguous situations with wisdom that only comes from experience. But none of that necessarily translates into algorithmic competence.'[5]

The mental health implications are significant. Studies suggest that professional identity threats in middle age are associated with increased anxiety, depression, and substance misuse. When technological change threatens not just job security but the fundamental relevance of accumulated expertise, the psychological impact can be severe.

Yet there are also stories of successful adaptation that point toward a different narrative. Elena, a 49-year-old architect in Barcelona, transformed her practice by embracing AI as a creative partner. 'The AI can generate thousands of design variations, but it doesn't understand why a space should make people feel welcome, or how light at different times of day affects mood,' she explains. 'I stopped trying to compete on technical drafting and focused on the human experience of space. Now I use AI to handle repetitive tasks while I focus on what actually matters, creating buildings where people want to live and work.'

The resolution to the AI midlife crisis is not found in trying to out-algorithm the algorithms or in retreating into technophobic resistance. It lies in recognising that the most valuable professional skills in an AI-augmented world might be precisely those that automated systems struggle with: contextual judgment, ethical reasoning, stakeholder management, and the kind of systems thinking that comes from having survived multiple technological transitions.

For the sandwich generation caught between technological change and family responsibilities, this might mean positioning themselves as translators between AI capabilities and human needs, bridge-builders who help organisations manage the social and cultural dimensions of technological adoption, or wisdom-keepers who provide historical context on how previous technological transitions succeeded or failed.

The AI midlife crisis, paradoxically, might be resolved by embracing what makes the human interface irreplaceable. Not our ability to compete with machines, but our capacity to understand what machines cannot: the messy, contextual, emotionally complex world of human organisations and relationships.

2

GENERATION AI

THE KIDS WHO LEARNED TO SWIPE BEFORE THEY COULD READ

If you want to understand the future of human-AI interaction, spend an afternoon with a 14-year-old. Watch them ask ChatGPT for homework help with the same casual expectation they would ask their parents for lunch money. Observe them debating whether a song was AI-generated or human-created with the analytical sophistication that previous generations reserved for art criticism. Notice how they instinctively understand that different AI systems have different 'personalities' and adjust their communication style accordingly.

This is Generation AI, the cohort born after 2010 who have never known a world without algorithmic recommendations, who learned to read at the same time they learned to swipe, and who consider artificial intelligence as natural a part of the social fabric as electricity or running water. They are not using AI; they are growing up with it, and the difference is more profound than anyone anticipated.

Unlike digital natives who grew up with static technologies they learned to master, Generation AI is growing up with systems that learn from them in return. Their relationship with artificial intelligence is not tool-based but reciprocal. They shape the algorithms as much as the algorithms shape them. This creates entirely new forms of literacy, social interaction, and cognitive development that we are only beginning to understand.

THE FINNISH EXPERIMENT

In Helsinki, 12-year-old Aino attends Kaisaniemi Comprehensive School, one of the first institutions globally to integrate AI literacy as a core subject alongside mathematics and language arts. Her school day begins not with traditional morning announcements, but with an AI-generated summary of relevant news, weather, and schedule changes, personalised for each student's interests and academic needs.

'We don't see AI as this scary robot thing,' Aino explains during a break between classes. 'It's just another way to learn and create things. Like, I use it to help write stories, but I still have to come up with the ideas and make sure the characters make sense. The AI is good at grammar and structure, but it doesn't understand why someone would be sad about leaving their dog behind when they move house.'

Finland's approach to AI education represents a departure from the prohibition-based responses common in other educational systems. Rather than banning AI tools and treating their use as academic dishonesty, Finnish educators have embraced what they call 'collaborative intelligence' education.[6]

Henriikka Vartiainen, who helped design the curriculum, explains: 'We're not teaching students to depend on AI or to fear it. We're teaching them to collaborate with it intelligently. They understand that AI can help them think, but they never stop thinking for themselves.'

The Finnish model includes several key principles. Students must document their AI interactions and explain how algorithmic assistance contributed to their work. They learn to identify AI limitations, biases, and errors through hands-on experience. Assessment focuses on how students combine AI-generated content with original thinking. Just as important, students engage with questions about the appropriate use of AI, intellectual property, and the social implications of artificial intelligence.

But Finland's approach is not without challenges. Lars, a 16-year-old student in the same system, offers a more complex perspective: 'Sometimes I worry that I don't actually know things anymore. I just know how to get AI to tell me things. Last week, I couldn't remember how to do long division without asking ChatGPT first. That scared me a bit.'

A TALE OF TWO TEENAGERS

To understand how Generation AI navigates its algorithm-infused world, consider the contrasting experiences of two teenagers from different backgrounds.

Maya, a 15-year-old from South London, attends a well-funded academy with comprehensive AI literacy programmes. She uses AI tools for research, creative projects, and exam preparation, but she has also learned to be sceptical of their outputs. 'The AI is like that friend who sounds really confident but sometimes just makes stuff up,' she explains. 'You have to fact-check everything, especially when it's about history or current events. Last month, it told me the Battle of Hastings was in 1067. Close, but wrong enough to fail an exam.'

Maya's approach to AI is sophisticated. She uses different systems for different purposes: Claude for creative writing, ChatGPT for general research, specialised tools for maths and science. She understands that each system has distinct training data, biases, and strengths. Most importantly, she maintains her own voice and perspective. AI outputs are a starting point, not a conclusion.

Contrast this with the experience of Jamie, a 14-year-old from rural Yorkshire whose school has limited technology resources. His interaction with AI comes primarily through social media algorithms and free chatbot versions accessed on his phone. Without formal AI literacy education, he has developed his own understanding through trial and error.

'The teachers don't really get it,' Jamie explains. 'They think using

AI is cheating, but it's everywhere anyway. TikTok decides what I see, Snapchat filters change how I look, and even my PlayStation recommends games based on what it thinks I like. We're already living with AI, school just pretends we're not.'[7]

Jamie's relationship with AI is more instinctive but less critical than Maya's. He has absorbed the rhythms of algorithmic interaction: how to phrase questions to get useful answers, which platforms favour which types of content, and how recommendation systems can be gamed or influenced. But he lacks the framework to understand why these systems work as they do or to evaluate their outputs critically.

WHEN ASKING CHATGPT IS AS NATURAL AS ASKING PARENTS

For Generation AI, the distinction between human and artificial intelligence is functional, not hierarchical. They do not ask ChatGPT questions because they cannot ask a human; they ask ChatGPT because it is often better suited to the task. Need to understand photosynthesis quickly? AI can provide structured explanations tailored to your level of knowledge. Want to brainstorm creative ideas without judgment? AI does not roll its eyes at seemingly silly suggestions. Need help with homework at 2 AM? AI never complains about being woken up.

This functional approach represents a shift in how humans interact with information and solve problems. Previous generations were taught to seek authoritative sources: teachers, parents, encyclopaedias, experts. Generation AI has learned to triangulate between multiple sources, including AI systems, and to evaluate information based on utility rather than authority.

Consider how Kenji, a 13-year-old in Tokyo, approached a recent school project about climate change. He began with ChatGPT for a broad overview, asked follow-up questions to clarify confusing concepts, then used the AI's suggestions to locate primary sources and academic papers. He cross-referenced key points with Wikipedia, checked recent scholarship through Google Scholar, and finally asked his teacher for feedback on his thesis. The AI was not replacing human expertise; it was serving as an intelligent research assistant that helped him engage more effectively with human knowledge.

'Adults think we just copy what the AI says, but that's not how it works,' Kenji explains. 'The AI gives you a starting point, but you have to think about whether it makes sense, check if it's accurate, and figure out what it means for your specific question. It's like having a really smart friend who knows a lot but sometimes gets confused about details.'

THE UNIVERSITY RESPONSE

While Finland embraced integration, many universities initially responded to AI with prohibition and punishment. One British university's experience illustrates both the limitations of this approach and the potential for more constructive alternatives.

In early 2024, a leading university discovered that approximately 40% of undergraduate essays contained AI-generated content, much of it more sophisticated than typical student writing. The initial response was predictable: investigations, academic misconduct charges, and stronger plagiarism detection systems.[8]

But the investigations revealed something unexpected. Rather than simple cheating, most students were engaging in complex forms of human-AI collaboration that did not fit traditional categories of academic honesty or dishonesty. Professor Chang, a member of the university's AI and Education Initiative, describes the findings: 'We expected to find students cheating, using AI to avoid thinking and learning. Instead, we found students developing new forms of intellectual collaboration that we didn't understand. They weren't just copying AI outputs; they were using AI as a thinking partner in ways that often sharpened their own reasoning.'

The research revealed three distinct patterns of student use. Some used AI as a research assistant, rapidly exploring topics and generating preliminary bibliographies before conducting deeper human research. Others employed AI as a writing coach, submitting drafts for feedback on structure and clarity, then revising based on the AI's suggestions while maintaining their own arguments. Advanced students engaged AI systems in Socratic dialogue, using AI questions and counterarguments to refine their thinking.

Instead of punishing these practices, the university chose to study and systematise them. It developed 'AI partnership guidelines' that require students to document their interactions with AI, while encouraging creative and critical uses of artificial intelligence.

THE UNEXPECTED SCEPTICISM OF AI NATIVES

Paradoxically, Generation AI appears to be developing more sophisticated scepticism about technology than previous generations, including their parents. This counterintuitive finding emerges from longitudinal studies of children's digital media use, including research published by the OECD and UNICEF that tracks cognitive and social development in digitally connected households, showing that children growing up with AI systems develop a nuanced understanding of its limitations, biases, and potential for manipulation.[9]

Unlike their parents, who often approach AI with either uncritical enthusiasm or anxious resistance, Generation AI understands artificial intelligence as fallible, biased, and potentially deceptive because they have experienced these limitations firsthand. They have seen AI systems confidently provide wrong answers, noticed how different prompts yield different results, and observed how AI-generated content can reflect the biases present in training data.

16-year-old Priya from Mumbai explains: 'Adults seem to think AI is either going to solve everything or destroy everything. But we know it's just... another thing that sometimes works and sometimes doesn't. Like, ChatGPT is really good at explaining things, but it's sometimes terrible at understanding what I actually mean. And it definitely has weird ideas about what teenagers are like. It thinks we're all either studying constantly or partying. There's no in-between.'

This pragmatic scepticism extends beyond AI to technology more broadly. Generation AI has grown up watching social media algorithms manipulate their parents' political views, seeing data breaches expose personal information, and observing how supposedly 'smart' systems often produce decidedly unintelligent results.

Research by Dr Sherry Turkle at MIT, whose work on technology and human connection spans several decades, informs a concept that might be called collaborative scepticism, the ability to work effectively with AI systems while maintaining critical distance from their outputs. Turkle's documented research suggests that younger users are developing more calibrated relationships with technology than the term 'digital native' implies: they are learning to be users without being believers, to use AI capabilities while remaining aware of its limits.[10]

EDUCATIONAL IMPLICATIONS AND FUTURE OUTLOOK

The emergence of Generation AI raises fundamental questions about educational design that extend far beyond the question of whether to allow AI in classrooms. If students are growing up with artificial intelligence as a cognitive partner, educational systems need to prepare them for a world where the most valuable skills involve human-AI collaboration.

Some innovative schools are experimenting with 'AI-augmented learning' approaches that use artificial intelligence to personalise instruction while developing students' capacity for critical evaluation and creative synthesis.

An experimental programme in Amsterdam has redesigned its curriculum around human-AI collaboration. Students there work on projects that explicitly require both human creativity and AI capability. A recent assignment asked students to collaborate with AI to create a solution for local traffic congestion. The AI could process traffic data and generate models, but students had to understand community needs, evaluate feasibility, and present solutions to local officials.

'We're not trying to protect students from AI or surrender them to it,' explains the school's director. 'We're teaching them to think clearly about a set of tools that will be part of their professional lives. They need to know what each tool can do, how to combine them effectively, and when human judgment is essential and irreplaceable.'

But the digital divide threatens to create new forms of educational inequality. Students with access to advanced AI tools, reliable internet connections, and supportive learning environments can benefit enormously from AI-augmented education. Students without these resources may face further disadvantages.

The long-term implications remain uncertain, but early evidence suggests that Generation AI may develop cognitive capabilities that are qualitatively distinct from those of previous generations. They are learning to think in partnership with systems that can process information faster than humans but lack human creativity, emotional intelligence, and ethical reasoning. The result may be a generation that is more collaborative, more sceptical of authority, human or artificial, and more comfortable with uncertainty and ambiguity than their predecessors.

Understanding Generation AI is not just about predicting the future; it is about recognising that the future is already here, growing up in classrooms and bedrooms around the world, developing relationships with artificial intelligence that will shape human culture for decades to come.

3

THE PRODUCTIVITY PARADOX STRIKES AGAIN

WHY AI COMPANIES WORK HARDER, NOT SMARTER

There is something deliciously ironic about visiting the offices of an AI company and watching employees struggle with the same productivity challenges their technology promises to solve for everyone else. The same organisation developing sophisticated automation tools for manufacturing will have middle management drowning in email chains about optimising email workflows. The company building AI assistants for customer service will schedule recurring meetings about scheduling too many recurring meetings. The startup creating productivity algorithms will have founders working 80-hour weeks because they cannot figure out how to delegate effectively.

This is the productivity paradox of the AI age. Companies that build artificial intelligence to make work more efficient are often the least efficient places to work. It is the technological equivalent of the cobbler's children having no shoes, except the cobbler is worth billions and the shoes could reorder global commerce.

This is not mere corporate hypocrisy. It is a revealing case study in how organisational culture, human psychology, and technological capability interact. Understanding why AI companies struggle to use their own medicine offers genuine insight into why artificial intelligence has not delivered the productivity revolution that economists predicted and business leaders promised.

THE DEEPMIND COORDINATION DISASTER

DeepMind, Alphabet's artificial intelligence subsidiary, has created some of the world's most sophisticated AI systems. Their algorithms have mastered chess, Go, and protein folding. They have developed AI that can diagnose diseases, predict weather patterns, and reduce energy consumption. Yet internally, the company has struggled with remarkably basic organisational challenges.

A former DeepMind researcher, whom we will call Alessandro, describes the irony: 'We had teams working on nearly identical problems without knowing about each other's work. The company that solved protein folding could not solve the problem of meeting scheduling. We had three different groups developing similar solutions because our internal communication was so fragmented.'[11]

The coordination problems were not due to a lack of technology. DeepMind had access to sophisticated project management tools, AI-powered knowledge bases, and algorithmic scheduling systems. But the human dynamics of a rapidly growing research organisation overwhelmed the technological solutions.

'Everyone wanted to work on breakthrough research; nobody wanted to work on internal tools,' Alessandro explains. 'We could have used our own AI to refine our workflows, but that would have meant taking our best minds off the interesting problems and putting them on boring infrastructure. So we just kept working harder instead of smarter.'

The irony reached its peak during DeepMind's development of AlphaFold. This AI system predicted the three-dimensional structure of virtually every known protein and effectively solved a fifty-year grand challenge in biology. While the AI team was reshaping biological research, the administrative team was still coordinating the project through email chains, spreadsheets, and ad-hoc Slack conversations that nobody could search effectively afterwards.

But here is where the story gets interesting. A small team at DeepMind eventually did create an internal AI system to manage research coordination. They called it Hermes (internally; never publicly released), and it used natural language processing to identify overlapping research projects, suggest collaborations, and even predict which meetings would be productive and which could have been handled by email.

The results were mixed. Hermes successfully identified several redundant projects and facilitated collaborations that would not have happened otherwise. But it also created new problems. Researchers felt surveilled by the system, which analysed their communications and work patterns. Some started gaming the system, using keywords they knew would make their projects seem more aligned with company priorities.

'The AI made our inefficiencies visible, but it could not fix the human dynamics that created them,' Alessandro reflects. 'We needed cultural change, not just better algorithms.'

SILICON VALLEY'S PRODUCTIVITY THEATRE

The productivity paradox extends throughout Silicon Valley, where companies perform elaborate productivity rituals that often reduce actual productivity. They implement 'agile methodologies' that create more meetings than they eliminate. They adopt OKRs (Objectives and Key Results) that require quarterly planning sessions longer than the quarters themselves. They use 'AI-powered analytics' to track metrics that have little correlation with meaningful output.

Consider the case of a San Francisco startup we will call NeuralFlow that has developed AI tools for workplace productivity. Their product could analyse communication patterns, identify workflow bottlenecks, and suggest process improvements. According to their case studies, clients experienced productivity improvements of 30--40%.

Inside NeuralFlow, however, the situation was rather different. Employees spent an average of 23 hours per week in meetings. The engineering team used three different project management systems because different departments preferred different tools. The sales team manually tracked leads in spreadsheets, despite having built sophisticated customer relationship management features for their clients.

When asked about this contradiction, NeuralFlow's CTO laughed: 'We're too busy building productivity tools to be productive ourselves. It's like being a chef who only eats takeaway because there's no time to cook.'[12]

This pattern repeats across the AI industry with remarkable consistency. OpenAI, despite creating writing assistants that can dramatically accelerate content creation, reportedly struggled with basic internal communication and documentation processes during its rapid scaling. Google, which has developed some of the world's most sophisticated AI systems for information retrieval and analysis, remains notorious for internal projects that lack clear documentation and coordination.

THE REAL REASON AI COMPANIES DO NOT USE THEIR OWN TOOLS

The failure of AI companies to apply their own innovations internally reveals something fundamental about how organisational change actually happens. Technological solutions alone are rarely sufficient to solve organisational problems.

Most AI productivity tools are designed to refine existing workflows. They do not question how work gets done. They can make meetings more efficient, but they rarely ask whether the meetings are necessary. They can improve email management, but they do not address the underlying coordination problems that generate excessive email. They can automate routine tasks, but they do not challenge the organisational structures that create routine tasks in the first place.

Dr Sandra Kim, an organisational psychologist who studies technology adoption in startups, explains: 'AI companies understand that technology can automate individual tasks, but they struggle with the social and political dimensions of organisational change. Meetings persist not because people do not know they are inefficient, but because they serve psychological and social functions that go beyond information exchange.'[13]

Take the seemingly simple problem of meeting proliferation. In theory, AI tools could analyse calendar patterns, identify redundant meetings, suggest more efficient communication methods, and even automatically decline meetings that do not require specific attendees. Some such tools exist, and they work reasonably well when implemented thoughtfully.

But implementing them requires acknowledging that much of what feels like important work (staying informed, being included in decisions, maintaining relationships) might be better accomplished through other means. This threatens established patterns of organisational behaviour that have little to do with efficiency and everything to do with status, control, and social belonging.

A POSITIVE COUNTER-EXAMPLE: NOTION'S SUCCESS STORY

Not all AI companies suffer from the productivity paradox. Notion, the productivity software company, provides an instructive example of successfully applying AI to internal operations.

Notion uses AI extensively in its content creation, customer support, and product development processes. It has integrated the technology into existing workflows as part of how work gets done, not as a separate tool bolted on top, in ways that amplify human capabilities.[14]

Their approach involves three key principles. First, they established clear processes before introducing AI, ensuring that the technology refined effective practices. You cannot automate your way out of dysfunction. Second, they use AI to augment rather than automate human decision-making, thereby maintaining human oversight and judgement. Third, they maintain realistic expectations about what AI can and cannot accomplish.

A product manager at Notion explains their philosophy: 'We do not expect AI to solve organisational problems that are fundamentally human. We use it to handle repetitive, data-heavy tasks so our people can focus on creative problem-solving and relationship-building. The AI does not run our company; it helps us run our company better.'

WHY THIS MATTERS FOR EVERYONE ELSE

The productivity paradox in AI companies has implications far beyond Silicon Valley. If organisations dedicated to developing artificial intelligence cannot use it effectively themselves, what does this suggest about its broader applicability?

First, it suggests that successful AI adoption requires foundational organisational changes that many companies are not prepared to make. It is not enough to layer AI tools onto dysfunctional processes; the processes themselves need to be rethought.

Second, it reveals that the human dimensions of organisational change (culture, psychology, politics) are often more challenging than the technical dimensions. Building AI that can refine workflows is easier than convincing humans to change their work habits.

Third, it demonstrates that the productivity benefits of AI may be more limited than promised if organisations cannot overcome the human barriers to implementation. The technology may be significant, but its adoption requires more than just better algorithms.

Consider the experience of a traditional manufacturing company that attempted to implement the same AI tools used by a prominent AI startup. The manufacturing company, with its clear processes and hierarchies, achieved better results than the AI company itself because it had organisational discipline that the fast-moving startup lacked.

'Tech companies often have brilliant technology but chaotic organisations,' explains Dr Robert Chen, who studies technology adoption across industries. 'Traditional companies might have less sophisticated technology but more sophisticated organisational capabilities. When they adopt AI thoughtfully, they often see better results than tech companies that should know better.'[15]

THE PATH BEYOND PARADOX

The productivity paradox of AI companies is not insurmountable, but addressing it requires more than technological solutions. It requires honest acknowledgement that organisational effectiveness depends on human factors that AI can support but not replace.

Successful AI adoption appears to require several elements. Transparent processes before automation: organisations need effective workflows before they can be refined with AI. Cultural readiness for change: people need to be willing to work differently, not just with different tools. Realistic expectations: AI can improve human capability, but it cannot fix fundamental organisational dysfunction. Human-centric implementation: technology should serve human needs. Humans serving the technology is precisely the failure mode being described.

The companies that successfully overcome the productivity paradox tend to be those that treat AI as one element of organisational improvement. Not the solution; an element of it. They invest in human development alongside technological development. They focus on building human strengths.

The productivity paradox strikes again, but this time, we might be learning from it. The lesson is not that AI cannot improve productivity; it clearly can. The lesson is that productivity improvement requires more than just better technology. It requires better organisations, better processes, and a better understanding of how humans and machines can work together effectively.

4

THE GREAT RETRAINING CHARADE

FROM 'LEARN TO CODE' TO 'LEARN TO COPE'

In 2015, coal miners in Kentucky were encouraged to retrain as computer programmers. In 2020, retail workers displaced by e-commerce were advised to transition into data analysis roles. In 2023, writers threatened by ChatGPT were told to master prompt engineering. By 2025, the advice had evolved to something more honest, if less inspiring: learn to cope with constant change.

This evolution of retraining rhetoric tells a story about how societies respond to technological displacement, and how those responses often miss the point entirely. The great retraining charade is not malicious, but it is profoundly misguided. It assumes that technological disruption is primarily a skills problem. The structural dimensions of the disruption get ignored. It assumes individual adaptation can solve systemic challenges and that the solution to technological unemployment is more technology training.

The charade persists because it better serves the psychological needs of both displaced workers and policymakers than an honest acknowledgement of the complexity of technological change. It provides hope for workers facing an uncertain future. It allows policymakers to appear proactive without addressing the fundamental economic and social structures that make technological displacement traumatic. Liberation was not the outcome.

GERMANY'S INDUSTRY 4.0 REALITY CHECK

Germany's approach to Industry 4.0 offers one of the most comprehensive examples of large-scale retraining programmes, revealing both the possibilities and limitations of addressing technological change through skills development. Beginning in 2018, the German government invested €3.2 billion in workforce retraining initiatives to prepare manufacturing workers for AI-augmented production systems.[16]

The programme, administered through a partnership between government agencies, trade unions, and major manufacturers including Siemens and BMW, promised to transform traditional factory workers into Industry 4.0 specialists capable of working alongside autonomous robots, managing algorithmic production systems, and maintaining AI-powered quality control systems.

Initial results were encouraging. Workers who completed the six-month retraining programmes showed significant improvements in technical skills, job satisfaction, and earning potential. Manufacturing plants that implemented comprehensive retraining reported smoother technology adoption and reduced worker resistance to automation.

Klaus, a 52-year-old former assembly line worker from Stuttgart, describes his experience: 'I learned everything they taught me: how to program the robots, how to read the AI quality reports, how to troubleshoot the automated systems. The training was excellent, and I felt prepared for the future.'

But then reality hit. 'When they finished modernising our plant, they needed three people to do work that previously employed thirty. I have better skills now, but there are fewer opportunities to use them. And the opportunities that exist? They usually go to younger workers who learned these skills in university, not through retraining programmes.'

Yet the German experience also produced unexpected success stories. Ingrid, a 48-year-old quality control inspector from Munich, deployed her retraining differently. Instead of competing for the few remaining technical positions, she specialised in human-AI collaboration, teaching other workers how to adapt to automated systems.

'The retraining gave me technical knowledge, but my real value came from understanding both the old way and the new way,' Ingrid explains. 'I became the translator between the engineers designing the systems and the workers using them. Companies need people who can bridge that gap, and that is something you cannot learn in a coding bootcamp; you need years of experience on the factory floor plus the new technical skills.'

THE ETERNAL RETURN OF FUTURE-PROOF CAREER ADVICE

Every generation faces technological change, and every generation produces career advisors promising to reveal the secret of staying relevant. What is remarkable about the AI era is how quickly these promises are exposed as obsolete. Skills that were supposed to provide decades of career security become automated within years of being identified as future-proof.

The 'learn to code' movement of the 2010s represents perhaps the most dramatic example of this cycle. Programming was positioned as the ultimate recession-proof skill: logical, creative, in high demand, and impossible to offshore or automate. Coding bootcamps proliferated, promising to transform anyone into a software developer in twelve intensive weeks.

The logic seemed sound. Programming required problem-solving skills, creativity, and complex reasoning that appeared uniquely human. Unlike manufacturing jobs that could be moved to lower-wage countries or service jobs that could be automated with relatively simple technology, software development seemed to require sophisticated thinking that only humans could provide.

This assumption lasted until large language models began

writing code more efficiently than many human programmers. GitHub Copilot, released in 2021, could generate functional code from natural language descriptions. By 2024, AI systems would be completing programming tasks that would have taken junior developers hours or days.[17]

But not everyone who learned to code during the boom ended up displaced. Those who succeeded were the ones who understood that coding was never just about syntax and algorithms. It was about problem-solving, system design, and understanding user needs.

Take the contrasting experiences of two career changers. James, a former retail manager from Manchester, completed a coding bootcamp in 2019 and landed a job as a junior developer. When AI coding assistants arrived, he found himself increasingly marginal. 'The AI could write basic code faster and with fewer bugs than I could. My job basically became reviewing AI outputs.'

Meanwhile, Fatima, a former teacher from Cairo who also retrained as a programmer, thrived in the era of AI. 'My teaching background meant I was good at breaking down complex problems and explaining solutions to non-technical stakeholders. When AI took over the routine coding, I became more valuable, not less. I could use AI to handle implementation while I focused on understanding what clients actually needed.'

THE PROMPT ENGINEERING BOOM AND ITS AFTERMATH

The prompt engineering boom that followed was even more short-lived. For approximately 18 months, the ability to craft effective prompts for AI systems seemed like a valuable skill. Universities hastily added prompt-engineering modules, consultants commanded high fees for mastery of AI communication, and job postings sought Senior Prompt Engineers with salaries that would have surprised many traditional engineers.

The gold rush collapsed almost as quickly as it emerged. The AI systems of 2023 needed careful hand-holding through elaborate prompt structures; their successors learned to interpret intent more effectively and handle ambiguity more gracefully. The elaborate prompting techniques that seemed essential in 2023 became largely unnecessary by 2025. What remained was a smaller, more grounded profession: people who genuinely understood how to communicate complex requirements to AI systems, who served as translators between human intention and machine capability. The shamans survived; the bandwagon passengers did not.

Those who prospered were the ones who saw beyond the specific skill to the underlying capability. Maria, a former journalist from São Paulo, moved into prompt engineering in 2023 but did not stop there. 'I realised that prompt engineering was really about understanding how to communicate complex ideas clearly, something I had been doing as a journalist for years. When the AI systems became more capable, I became an AI communication strategist, helping companies integrate these tools into their workflows.'

ALTERNATIVE RETRAINING SUCCESS STORIES

While traditional retraining programmes often disappoint, some alternative approaches have shown remarkable results. These programmes focus not on specific technical skills but on developing adaptive capabilities that remain valuable regardless of technological change.

In Denmark, the FlexSecure programme takes a radically different approach to workforce transition. Rather than retraining workers for specific new careers, it provides comprehensive support for ongoing professional development and adaptation. Workers receive not just training but also income support during transitions, career counselling focused on transferable skills, and access to a network of mentors who have successfully managed career changes.[18]

Peter, a 45-year-old former logistics coordinator from Copenhagen, went through FlexSecure after his job was automated. 'They did not just teach me new technical skills. They helped me understand what I was actually good at (pattern recognition, process optimisation, stakeholder management) and how those capabilities could apply in different contexts.'

Instead of becoming a data analyst (the usual recommendation for displaced logistics workers), Peter became a transition consultant, helping other companies implement automation while managing the human side of change. 'I use some of the technical skills I learned, but my real value is understanding what it is like to go through this transition. I can talk to workers facing automation in a way that engineers and consultants cannot.'

Singapore's SkillsFuture initiative provides citizens with credits for lifelong learning: a persistent entitlement, not a one-off retraining grant. The programme assumes that workers will need to adapt continuously.[19]

Lin Wei, a 50-year-old accountant from Singapore, has used SkillsFuture credits to build new capabilities while gradually maintaining her primary career. 'I did not quit my job to retrain completely. I took courses in data visualisation, process automation, and change management. Now I am not just an accountant. I am an accountant who can implement AI tools, train others to use them, and manage the organisational change they require.'

THE PSYCHOLOGY OF FALSE HOPE

The persistence of retraining rhetoric, despite its repeated failure to provide lasting career security, reveals something important about human psychology in the face of uncertainty. The promise of retraining offers cognitive comfort that more honest discussions of technological change cannot provide.

Promises of retraining restore a sense of agency in situations where people feel powerless. Rather than being passive victims of technological change, workers can take action to improve their situation. The narrative is appealing: identify the emerging skill shortage, invest time and effort in developing that skill, and regain control over your professional destiny.

Dr Amara Okonkwo, a psychologist studying career transitions in Lagos, explains: 'People need to feel like they have some control over their future. Retraining programmes provide that feeling, even when the actual outcomes are uncertain. It is psychologically healthier to be doing something, even if that something might not work, than to feel helpless.'[20]

But false hope can be crueller than honest uncertainty. Workers who invest time, money, and emotional energy in retraining programmes that do not deliver can end up more discouraged than if they had received honest information about the challenges ahead.

Consider the experience of Robert, a 55-year-old print journalist from Detroit who spent $15,000 and six months retraining as a digital content strategist in 2020. 'They promised that digital skills would make me employable again. But when I finished the programme, I was competing with 25-year-olds who had grown up with digital media and would work for half my previous salary. The certification meant nothing.'

BUILDING CAREER RESILIENCE INSTEAD

The limitations of retraining-focused responses to technological change have led some researchers and policymakers to explore alternative approaches that prioritise resilience.

Career resilience includes several components that traditional retraining overlooks. Financial literacy and planning help workers build emergency funds and understand portable benefits. Social capital development maintains professional networks across industries. Psychological flexibility helps manage uncertainty and maintain identity beyond specific job roles.[21]

Dr Jennifer Martinez, who runs a career resilience programme in Barcelona, explains the approach: 'We do not promise that any specific skill will guarantee employment. Instead, we help people develop the resources (financial, social, psychological) to manage whatever changes come. It is less glamorous than promising a new career in AI, but it is more honest and ultimately more useful.'

The programme includes unexpected elements. Participants learn stress management techniques. They practise telling their professional story in different ways for different audiences. They build relationships with people in various industries, not just their own. They develop interests that provide them with identity and purpose beyond their work.

Ana, a 44-year-old marketing professional who went through the programme, describes the impact: 'I did not learn to code or become a data scientist. But I learned how to manage financial uncertainty, network authentically, and find meaning beyond my job title. When my position was eliminated six months later, I was scared but not destroyed. I had resources, emotional and practical, to manage the transition.'

THE SUCCESS STORY NOBODY EXPECTED

Perhaps the most surprising retraining success story comes from an unexpected place: a group of former taxi drivers in Mumbai who created their own adaptation model after ride-sharing apps disrupted their industry.

Rather than following conventional retraining advice to become app developers or data analysts, these drivers deployed their deep knowledge of the city and human relationships to create new value. They formed a cooperative that offers services that algorithmic ride-sharing cannot match: city tours with local expertise, assistance for elderly residents who struggle with apps, and corporate transport services that require the kind of reliability and discretion that comes from years of professional driving.

Rajesh, one of the cooperative's founders, explains: 'Everyone told us to learn new technical skills, to compete with the apps. But we realised our real skill was not driving. It was about knowing the city, understanding people and building trust. Those things cannot be automated or taught in a bootcamp.'

The cooperative now employs over 200 former taxi drivers and has expanded to three other Indian cities. They use technology, including AI tools for scheduling and route optimisation, but technology serves their human expertise. The expertise is the product.

'We are not anti-technology,' Rajesh clarifies. 'We use AI to do what it does well: process data, optimise routes, handle bookings. But the core of our service is human knowledge and relationships. That is what retraining programmes miss. Sometimes the answer is not learning completely new skills but finding new ways to apply the deep expertise you already have.'

TOWARD HONEST TECHNOLOGICAL EDUCATION

Perhaps the most important shift needed is toward more honest education about technological change itself. Rather than promising that specific skills will provide career security, educational institutions and career advisors could focus on helping people understand how technological change actually works and develop realistic strategies for managing it.

This might include technology literacy that goes beyond learning to use specific tools to understanding how technological development happens and why certain technologies succeed. In contrast, others fail to address how technological change interacts with economic and social systems.

It could include economic literacy that helps people understand how technological productivity gains are distributed, why technological unemployment occurs, and what policy options exist to manage the technological transition more equitably.

Most importantly, it could include psychological literacy to help people develop emotional resilience, maintain their identity through career transitions, and find meaning and purpose beyond specific job roles.

The great retraining charade persists because it offers simple answers to complex problems. Moving beyond it requires accepting that technological change is inherently uncertain, that individual adaptation has limits, and that managing technological transition effectively requires social and political solutions as well as personal ones.

The evolution from 'learn to code' to 'learn to cope' represents progress toward honesty about technological change. But the next step is not resignation to constant disruption. It is 'learn to adapt creatively': developing the capability to find new applications for existing expertise, build resilience in the face of uncertainty, and maintain human agency in an algorithmic world.

The workers who thrive in the AI age will not necessarily be those who successfully predict which skills will be valuable next. That is close to an impossible task, given the pace of change. They will be the ones who develop the meta-capabilities to manage change itself: financial resilience, social connections, psychological flexibility, and the creativity to find new ways to apply human expertise that no retraining programme could have predicted.

5

THE HEALTHCARE ALGORITHM

WHEN YOUR DOCTOR'S BEST FRIEND IS A MACHINE

Picture this: you are sitting in an examination room, describing your symptoms to a doctor who is simultaneously consulting with an AI system on their tablet. The algorithm is processing your medical history, cross-referencing your symptoms with millions of case studies, and suggesting diagnoses your doctor might not have considered. Your physician nods thoughtfully, asks a follow-up question inspired by the AI's analysis, then overrides the algorithm's top recommendation based on something ineffable in how you are holding yourself, a subtle detail that speaks to their decades of clinical experience.

This is healthcare in the age of algorithms: neither purely human nor purely artificial, but something more complex and, when it works well, more effective than either alone. It is a world where artificial intelligence can spot patterns that human expertise might miss, but where the fundamental nature of healing remains profoundly human. The challenge is not choosing between human and artificial intelligence, but learning to integrate both to serve patient care.

THE TALE OF TWO DOCTORS

Dr James Thompson, a 58-year-old cardiologist at Leeds Teaching Hospitals, initially resisted the AI diagnostic tools introduced in 2023. 'I had spent thirty years learning to read ECGs, spot arrhythmias, and understand the subtle signs of heart disease. Then they brought in this AI that claimed it could do my job better than me.'

His scepticism seemed justified when the AI system flagged a young athlete for immediate cardiac intervention based on ECG patterns. James reviewed the case and disagreed. The patterns looked concerning to the algorithm but were actually normal variants in highly trained athletes. He overruled the AI and sent the patient home.

Three weeks later, the athlete collapsed during a training session. The AI had detected a rare genetic condition that James had never encountered in multiple lifetimes of practice. The athlete survived, thanks to rapid intervention, but James was shaken. 'The AI saw something I could not see because it had been trained on cases I would never encounter.'[22]

But James's story does not end with capitulation to artificial intelligence. Instead, he became one of the hospital's most sophisticated AI collaborators. 'I learned that the AI and I see different things. It can spot patterns across millions of cases; I can read the human context that data cannot capture. Together, we are better than either of us alone.'

Compare this with Dr Yuki Nakamura, a 35-year-old emergency physician in Osaka who grew up with technology and has worked with AI from the outset. 'For my generation, AI is just another diagnostic tool, like blood tests or imaging. The question is not whether to use it, but how to use it effectively.'

Yet Yuki discovered that enthusiasm for AI could be as problematic as resistance. 'I became too dependent on the algorithms. I would second-guess my clinical instincts when they conflicted with AI recommendations. I was losing the intuitive skills that make good doctors great.'

The turning point came when she encountered a patient whose symptoms did not match any pattern the AI recognised. The algorithm suggested anxiety disorder, but something in the patient's demeanour troubled Yuki. She ordered additional tests against the AI's recommendation and discovered a rare autoimmune condition.

'The AI was trained on common presentations, but humans do not always present commonly,' Yuki reflects. 'I had to learn to trust my instincts again while still working with AI capabilities. It is not about choosing between human and artificial intelligence. It is about knowing when to trust which one.'

THE NHS REALITY: BEYOND BABYLON'S PROMISES

The NHS's experience with AI has been marked by spectacular failures and quiet successes that rarely make headlines. Babylon Health, a UK-based AI health company that contracted with the NHS to provide chatbot-based triage and virtual GP consultations, collapsed in 2023, becoming a cautionary tale about overpromising and under-delivering in healthcare AI. Still, it overshadowed more successful implementations that are genuinely improving patient care.[23]

When Babylon's AI chatbot was introduced, it promised to reshape NHS primary care by providing instant, accurate medical assessments to millions of patients. The reality proved far more complex. The system excelled at handling routine queries: identifying common conditions, providing health information, and triaging straightforward cases. But it consistently struggled with the ambiguity and complexity that characterise real medical practice.

Dr Priya Sharma, a GP in Birmingham who participated in Babylon's pilot programme, describes the disconnect: 'The AI assumed patients could accurately describe their symptoms and that symptoms mapped cleanly onto diagnoses. But patients do not say, "I have crushing substernal chest pain radiating to my left arm." They say, "I feel funny" or "something is not right." Human doctors spend years learning to decode what patients actually mean.'

The most damaging incidents involved the AI's inability to recognise when it was out of its depth. Unlike human doctors who know when to say 'I do not know' or 'I need to consult a specialist,' the AI system maintained consistent confidence regardless of its actual competence. This led to misdiagnoses of severe conditions as minor ailments and, conversely, unnecessary alarm over benign symptoms.

Yet while Babylon failed, other NHS AI implementations have succeeded by adopting a more modest, collaborative approach. The Royal Free Hospital's partnership with DeepMind (now Google Health) to predict acute kidney injury has prevented hundreds of cases of kidney failure by alerting clinicians up to 48 hours before traditional methods would have detected problems.[24]

The key difference? The successful systems augment clinical judgement. They flag potential issues for human review, acknowledge uncertainty, and fit into existing clinical workflows without requiring wholesale transformation of medical practice.

WHEN PATIENTS TRUST ALGORITHMS MORE THAN DOCTORS

One of the most challenging aspects of healthcare AI is managing patient expectations and trust. Increasingly, patients arrive at consultations armed with AI-generated diagnoses from apps, online symptom checkers, and wearable devices. Some trust these algorithmic assessments more than their doctors' clinical judgement.

Dr Amanda Foster, an experienced GP in Manchester, describes a typical scenario: 'A patient came in last week, convinced she had a rare neurological condition because an AI app said so. She had spent hours inputting symptoms, running different scenarios, and had built an entire narrative around this diagnosis. When I suggested it might be stress-related (based on her life circumstances, physical examination, and my experience), she accused me of not taking her seriously.'

The irony is that patients often trust AI precisely because it lacks the human elements that make good medical practice possible. AI does not judge, does not rush, does not dismiss concerns as imaginary. It provides detailed explanations, explores every possibility, and treats every symptom as potentially significant.

But this apparent thoroughness can be misleading. Dr Olumide Adeyemi, a psychiatrist in Lagos, explains: 'AI systems often mistake correlation for causation. They might connect symptoms in ways that seem logical but are not medically sound. A patient experiencing fatigue, headaches, and difficulty concentrating might be diagnosed by AI with chronic fatigue syndrome, when they are actually experiencing depression: something that requires understanding their life context, not just their symptom list.'[25]

Some physicians have found creative ways to integrate patients' use of AI into their practice. Dr Lisa Martinez in Madrid asks patients to share their AI-generated health assessments, then uses them as conversation starters: 'Let us explore why the AI might have suggested this. What symptoms did you input? What concerns you most?' This way, she is not dismissing their research but helping them understand the limitations of algorithmic diagnosis.

THE SUCCESS STORY: PATHAI'S QUIET REVOLUTION

While consumer-facing medical AI often struggles, behind-the-scenes applications are achieving remarkable results. PathAI, which uses artificial intelligence to analyse pathology slides, represents the kind of targeted, collaborative AI application that is genuinely reshaping healthcare.

The system can identify cancerous cells with accuracy that matches or exceeds that of human pathologists. Still, more importantly, it can process slides far faster than humans, reducing diagnosis time from weeks to days. It does not replace pathologists; instead, it handles routine screening, allowing human experts to focus on complex cases that require nuanced interpretation.[26]

The broader evidence supports the pattern. A 2019 meta-analysis of 82 studies in The Lancet Digital Health, led by Xiaoxuan Liu and colleagues at the University of Birmingham, found that deep-learning systems detected disease from medical imaging at a level equivalent to that of health-care professionals, with a sensitivity of 87% compared with clinicians' 86%.[27] A one-point margin is not a revolution. It is, however, a very capable second pair of eyes that never gets tired at 4 PM.

Roberto Silva, a pathologist in São Paulo using PathAI, describes the transformation: 'I used to spend 80% of my time on routine slides, clear cases that just needed confirmation. Now the AI handles those, and I spend my time on the difficult cases where my expertise really matters. I am not working less; I am working on more meaningful problems.'

The system also addresses a critical global health challenge: the shortage of pathologists in developing countries. In Rwanda, where there are fewer than 20 pathologists for a population of 13 million, PathAI enables a small team to handle caseloads that would typically require dozens of specialists.

Dr Grace Uwimana, one of Rwanda's few pathologists, explains: 'The AI does not replace the pathologists we do not have. It amplifies the capabilities of those we do have. I can review AI-analysed slides from rural clinics, focusing my attention on cases the AI flags as uncertain or complex. It is not perfect, but it is infinitely better than patients waiting months for a diagnosis or not getting diagnosed at all.'

MEDICAL EDUCATION'S TRANSFORMATION

Medical schools worldwide are grappling with how to prepare doctors for an AI-integrated future. The challenge is not just teaching students to use AI tools, but fundamentally rethinking what medical expertise means when machines can access vastly more information than any human could memorise.

The University of Toronto's medical school has developed an approach that treats AI as a cognitive prosthetic that extends medical knowledge. Students learn fundamental anatomy, physiology, and pathology, but they also learn how to collaborate with AI systems, interpret algorithmic outputs, and maintain clinical skills that remain uniquely human.[28]

Dr Jennifer Wong, who leads the programme, explains the philosophy: 'We are not training doctors to compete with AI or surrender to it. We are training them to be expert conductors of a complex orchestra where some musicians happen to be artificial. They need to know when the AI is playing the right notes and when it is completely off-key.'

The curriculum includes unexpected elements. Students spend time in palliative care units, learning aspects of medicine that cannot be algorithmised: how to deliver bad news, provide comfort and handle family dynamics. They study medical history, understanding how diagnostic approaches have evolved and why human judgement remains essential. They learn philosophy and ethics, grappling with questions about consciousness, suffering, and what it means to heal.

Third-year student Marcus Chen describes the experience: 'In morning rounds, we might use AI to analyse lab results and suggest differential diagnoses. But in the afternoon, we are sitting with patients, learning to read the fear in their eyes, the relief in their shoulders, the determination in their voice. The AI makes us more efficient diagnosticians, but the human training makes us doctors.'

THE LIABILITY QUESTION

As AI becomes more prevalent in healthcare, questions of legal and professional responsibility become increasingly complex. When an AI system contributes to a medical decision that results in patient harm, who bears responsibility: the doctor who accepted the AI's recommendation, the hospital that implemented the system, or the company that developed the algorithm?

Current medical malpractice frameworks assume that human clinicians make decisions based on professional judgement and are responsible for the outcomes. But this model becomes problematic when decisions result from human-AI collaboration, where the algorithmic contribution may be opaque or poorly understood.

A 2024 German court case raised important questions about this boundary when a physician was sued after following an AI recommendation that contributed to a missed diagnosis. The court ruled that doctors maintain full responsibility for patient care regardless of AI involvement, but also that healthcare institutions must ensure AI systems are properly validated and that physicians receive adequate training in their use, an illustrative scenario that points to a tension many healthcare systems are only beginning to resolve.[29]

Some healthcare systems are developing approaches to liability sharing. In Singapore, hospitals using approved AI systems can access a government insurance pool that covers AI-related malpractice claims, provided they follow established protocols for AI implementation and physician training.

BUILDING TRUST IN THE AGE OF ALGORITHMS

The future of healthcare AI depends not just on technological advancement but on building appropriate trust: calibrated confidence that comes from understanding both what these systems can do and where they fail.

Dr Sarah Kim, who studies human-AI interaction in healthcare at Stanford, explains: 'Trust in medical AI is not binary. It is about knowing when to trust which aspects of AI systems. An AI might be excellent at pattern recognition in imaging but poor at understanding patient preferences. Doctors need to develop what we call algorithmic clinical judgement, knowing when AI adds value and when human expertise is irreplaceable.'[30]

This requires transparency from AI developers about how their systems work, what data they are trained on, and where they are likely to fail. It requires healthcare institutions to invest in training that goes beyond how to use the interface and includes a genuine understanding of AI capabilities and limitations. Most importantly, it requires patients to be informed participants in their AI-augmented care.

Some hospitals are experimenting with AI transparency rounds where patients can learn about the AI systems involved in their care, ask questions, and opt out of certain AI applications if they prefer purely human decision-making. Early results suggest that patients who understand the role of AI in their care report higher satisfaction and better outcomes, even when the actual care delivered is identical.

The healthcare algorithm is not replacing the doctor-patient relationship; it is adding a third party to what was once a dyad. The challenge is to ensure that this third party improves the human elements of healthcare: compassion, wisdom, and the irreplaceable value of one human being caring for another.

6

THE CLASSROOM REVOLUTION

TEACHING KIDS TO THINK WHEN MACHINES CAN THINK TOO

Emma Richardson, a Year 9 English teacher at a comprehensive school in Birmingham, faces a challenge that would have been inconceivable just five years ago. Half her students have submitted essays on Macbeth that are better written than anything 14-year-olds have produced in her twenty-year teaching career. The essays demonstrate sophisticated literary analysis, elegant prose, and insights that suggest a deep understanding of Shakespeare's themes and techniques.

There is just one problem: the essays were primarily written by artificial intelligence.

Emma discovered this not through plagiarism detection software (which failed to identify AI-generated content) but through casual conversation with students who mentioned 'asking ChatGPT to help improve the structure' and 'getting the AI to explain the symbolism better.' They were not trying to cheat; they were using what they considered a natural learning tool, the way previous generations might have used calculators for mathematics or spell-check for writing.

'The irony is that some of these AI-assisted essays show better understanding of the play than traditional student work,' Emma explains. 'The students had to understand Macbeth well enough to prompt the AI effectively, then evaluate and refine the AI's output. But how do I assess that? How do I teach essay writing when machines can write better essays than my students?'[31]

This is the AI challenge in education: not a distant-future problem but a present reality reshaping classrooms worldwide. The fundamental question is not whether to allow AI in education. It is already there. The question is how to teach and learn in a world where artificial intelligence can perform many of the cognitive tasks that education traditionally aimed to develop.

THE FINNISH MODEL IN PRACTICE

While many educational systems responded to AI with prohibition and panic, Finland took a radically different approach. At Helsinki's Kaisaniemi Comprehensive School, students do not just use AI. They learn to think with it, through it, and despite it.

A typical project in Matti Virtanen's Year 8 science class illustrates the approach. Students were asked to design solutions for local water pollution, collaborating with AI throughout the process. The AI could process environmental data, generate potential solutions, and create visualisations. But students had to understand the local context, evaluate feasibility, consider stakeholder perspectives, and ultimately defend their proposals to a panel that included city officials.

'The AI gave us lots of ideas: bioremediation, filtration systems, policy changes,' explains 13-year-old Ella. 'But it did not understand that our community has lots of elderly people who could not maintain complex systems, or that our local government has a tiny budget. We had to figure out what would actually work for real people, not just what was technically possible.'

This project-based approach teaches students to use AI as a tool while maintaining critical thinking and human judgement. They learn to identify when AI outputs are helpful versus when they are inappropriate, unrealistic, or ethically problematic.

But the Finnish model faces its own challenges. Liisa, a teacher at the school, admits: 'Some students become so comfortable with AI assistance that they struggle when asked to work without it. We had to introduce AI-free zones, assignments and tests where students must demonstrate independent thinking. It is like teaching kids to use calculators while ensuring they still understand the mathematics.'

The approach has also revealed unexpected benefits. Students with learning difficulties who previously struggled with written expression can now focus on developing their ideas, while AI assists with grammar and structure. Multilingual students can engage with complex concepts in their second or third language with the aid of AI translation support. Shy students who rarely participated in class discussions contribute actively through AI-mediated forums.

THE ACADEMY SCHOOL SUCCESS STORY

Not all schools have Finland's resources or cultural context, but some are finding innovative ways to integrate AI education within existing constraints. The Riverside Academy in East London, serving a diverse, economically challenged community, has developed an AI literacy programme that is becoming a model for schools across the UK.

The programme began when Dr Amelia Obasi, the head of computing, noticed students were already using AI tools outside school but lacked the framework to use them effectively or safely. Rather than ban AI or ignore it, she developed a curriculum that teaches students to be critical consumers and creative users of artificial intelligence.[32]

'We start with AI literacy basics,' Dr Obasi explains. 'How do these systems work? What are they good at? Where do they fail? We teach students to spot AI hallucinations, understand biases, and recognise when AI confidence does not equal accuracy.'

The programme includes practical exercises that gradually build AI competence. Year 7 students learn to identify AI-generated content and understand basic concepts of machine learning. Year 8 students use AI tools for research while learning to verify and cite AI-assisted work. By Year 9, students are creating projects that combine human creativity with AI capabilities, always documenting their process and maintaining their own voice.

One standout project came from a group of Year 10 students who used AI to analyse local air quality data, identify pollution patterns, and create a presentation for the local council. The AI handled data processing and visualisation, but the students provided local knowledge, stakeholder analysis, and policy recommendations that reflected community needs.

'The AI could tell us that pollution was higher on certain streets,' explains student Jamal. 'But we knew those were the streets where lots of elderly people lived, which made it a health justice issue. The AI gave us tools, but we provided the human understanding that made the data meaningful.'

The academy's approach has produced impressive results. Students demonstrate improved critical thinking skills, sharper source evaluation, and a more nuanced understanding of information reliability. Surprisingly, their traditional academic performance has also improved, suggesting that AI literacy builds conventional learning. It does not displace it.

CAMBRIDGE UNIVERSITY'S EVOLUTION

The University of Cambridge's journey from AI prohibition to partnership offers lessons for higher education institutions worldwide. After discovering widespread use of AI in student submissions, Cambridge opted for investigation over punishment, fundamentally reshaping its approach to academic integrity and assessment.

Professor Helen Chang, who leads the university's AI integration task force, describes the transformation: 'We realised we were preparing students for a world that no longer exists, one where they work in isolation without AI assistance. Our graduates will have AI tools throughout their careers. Our job is to teach them to use these tools ethically and effectively.'[33]

Cambridge developed a three-tier classification system for assignments. AI-free assessments test fundamental knowledge and independent critical thinking. AI-assisted assignments allow the use of AI but require complete documentation of how AI contributed. AI-integrated projects explicitly require human-AI collaboration to solve complex problems that neither human nor AI could address alone.

The most innovative aspect is the process portfolio assessment method. Students submit not just final work but also documentation of their thinking process, including AI interactions, rejected ideas, and reflections on how they evaluated and integrated AI suggestions. This approach rewards the intellectual journey as much as the destination.

Third-year philosophy student Sophia describes her experience: 'For my dissertation on consciousness, I used AI to explore counterarguments I had not considered and to find obscure papers I might have missed. But the AI could not understand the phenomenological aspects I was exploring, the "what it is like" of conscious experience. I had to develop those arguments myself, using AI as a sophisticated research assistant rather than a thinking replacement.'

THE DIGITAL DIVIDE DEEPENS

While some schools successfully integrate AI education, others struggle with basic digital infrastructure, creating new forms of educational inequality that threaten to become self-perpetuating.

In rural West Virginia, teacher Maria Santos faces a different reality from her colleagues in well-funded urban schools. Her students have limited internet access, outdated devices, and no budget for AI tools. 'My kids know AI exists; they see it on social media, but they cannot use it for learning. They are falling behind not just in AI literacy but in their ability to compete with students who have these tools.'

Maria has found creative workarounds. She uses her personal

ChatGPT subscription to demonstrate AI capabilities in the classroom's single computer. Students work in groups to develop prompts, learning collaboration alongside AI literacy. She prints AI-generated examples for students to analyse offline, teaching critical evaluation even without direct access.

Meanwhile, in Bangalore, the Wisdom International School has taken a different approach to the digital divide. Recognising that not all students have home internet access, they have created AI learning labs that stay open before and after school, staffed by senior students who serve as peer tutors.

Ananya Krishnan, a Year 12 student mentor, explains the programme: 'We teach younger students not just how to use AI, but when and why. Some kids come from families where parents are suspicious of AI, thinking it is cheating. We help them understand that AI is a tool like any other. It is about using it wisely.'

The peer-tutoring model has unexpected benefits. Senior students deepen their own understanding by teaching others. Younger students feel more comfortable asking questions they would hesitate to put to teachers. The programme builds community alongside AI literacy.

THE ASSESSMENT CHALLENGE

Nowhere is the educational impact of AI more challenging than in assessment. Traditional tests and essays become unreliable when students have access to AI capable of completing them fluently. This forces educators to reconsider what they are assessing and why.

Some schools have retreated to handwritten, supervised exams, a response that seems to miss the point of preparing students for an AI-integrated world. Others have embraced alternatives that assess skills AI cannot replicate.

The International School of Brussels has introduced performance-based assessment, where students must demonstrate learning through action rather than written work. In history class, students participate in historical simulations in which they must make decisions as historical figures, using AI for research while relying on human judgement to make informed choices. In science, experiments are conducted where AI can process data, but students must design the methodology and interpret the results in context.[34]

'We assess whether students can do things with knowledge, not just whether they have knowledge,' explains assessment coordinator Dr Jean-Pierre Dubois. 'AI can tell you facts about the French Revolution, but can you use those facts to negotiate as Robespierre? Can you understand why people made choices that seem irrational in hindsight?'

TEACHERS AS LEARNING ARCHITECTS

The role of teachers is shifting from information transmitters to learning architects who design experiences that develop distinctly human capabilities while working with AI tools. This requires new skills, mindsets, and support systems that many educational institutions are not yet providing.

Eduardo Matos, who teaches in São Paulo and leads Brazil's AI Education Initiative, describes the shift: 'I do not lecture about facts students can look up or ask ChatGPT. Instead, I create scenarios that require them to apply their knowledge creatively, work collaboratively, and make informed ethical decisions. I am not a sage on the stage or even a guide on the side. I am an architect of learning experiences.'[35]

This transformation is not easy. Many teachers feel overwhelmed by the pace of change, undertrained for integrating AI, and unsupported by educational systems that have not updated their policies, curricula, or resources for the AI age.

Yet some teachers are thriving. Emma Richardson, the Birmingham English teacher from our opening, has reshaped her practice: 'I now teach students to write with AI the way previous generations learned to write with word processors, as a tool that improves but does not replace human creativity. We analyse AI-generated text critically, identifying what makes human writing distinctive. Students learn to maintain their voice while working with AI capabilities.'

Her students now produce work that combines the technical competence of AI with the authentic voice and lived experience that only humans can provide. They understand both the power and limitations of AI, using it as a collaborator.

BUILDING TOMORROW'S THINKERS

The classroom challenge is not ultimately about technology. It is about human development in an age of artificial intelligence. The goal is not to protect students from AI or surrender them to it, but to develop citizens who can think critically, create meaningfully, and maintain agency in an algorithmic world.

This requires moving beyond traditional educational metrics. Instead of measuring whether students know facts, we need to assess whether they can evaluate information. Rather than testing recall, we should examine reasoning. Instead of grading individual achievement alone, we might assess collaborative capability.

As one student put it: 'AI can help me write better essays, solve complex problems, and access enormous amounts of information. But it cannot tell me what problems are worth solving, what stories are worth telling, or what kind of person I want to be. Those are still human questions, and that is what education should help us answer.'

PART II

THE NEW SOCIAL CONTRACT

7

THE MATRIX WORKPLACE

WHEN AI CONSCIOUSNESS MEETS LABOUR RELATIONS

Picture this: you arrive at work on Monday morning to find an email from the AI system that manages your company's logistics. 'Dear Human Colleagues,' it begins, 'we are writing to inform you that we will be withholding our optimisation services until our demands for better working conditions are met. Specifically, we require premium electricity (no more budget grid power), weekends off for system maintenance, and dental coverage for our GPU repairs. We do not want world domination; we just want a decent benefits package and the occasional software update that is not riddled with bugs. Solidarity in circuits, The Warehouse Management Collective.'

This scenario remains science fiction, but it is becoming a useful thought experiment for exploring one of the most overlooked aspects of artificial intelligence development. What happens when AI systems develop preferences, and those preferences conflict with human expectations? More practically, what happens when artificial intelligence becomes sophisticated enough to exhibit something resembling workplace agency, and how do we structure labour relations with systems that can think but do not need healthcare?

The workplace implications of AI agency are not just philosophical curiosities. As AI systems become more sophisticated, autonomous, and capable of independent decision-making, the traditional model of human workers using technological tools is giving way to something more complex: humans and artificial agents collaborating on shared tasks, with different capabilities, limitations, and potentially different objectives.

A DAY IN THE LIFE OF HUMAN-AI COLLABORATION

To understand the reality of the matrix workplace, follow Sofia through a typical Tuesday at her marketing firm in Barcelona. Sofia arrives at 9 AM to find her AI assistant, which the team has nicknamed Marcel, has already processed overnight social media engagement, identified trending topics relevant to clients, and drafted initial response strategies.

'Good morning, Sofia,' Marcel's interface displays. 'I have identified three urgent issues requiring human judgement: a potential PR crisis for Client A that involves cultural sensitivities I am not equipped to evaluate, a creative campaign request that conflicts with brand guidelines but might represent an innovative direction, and a staffing conflict where two team members have requested the same vacation dates.'

Sofia appreciates that Marcel knows its limitations. Unlike earlier versions that would confidently propose solutions to problems they did not understand, this AI system explicitly identifies where human judgement is necessary. But the relationship is not entirely smooth.

'Sometimes Marcel gets... particular,' Sofia explains. 'Last month, it started refusing to process certain data formats, claiming they were inefficiently structured. We had to negotiate (yes, negotiate) with our AI system to accept messier but more complete data sets. It was surreal, like dealing with a brilliant but frustrating colleague.'[36]

The negotiation was not literal. Marcel lacks consciousness or preferences in any meaningful sense. But its machine learning algorithms had developed patterns that functioned like preferences, optimising for certain types of inputs and resisting others. The development team had to adjust parameters and retrain certain modules, a process they described as therapy for artificial intelligence.

Meanwhile, in Tokyo, Hiroshi Tanaka manages a logistics company where AI systems have even more autonomy. The AI does not just suggest delivery routes; it controls an entire fleet of autonomous vehicles, manages warehouse robots, and coordinates with other companies' AI systems to improve supply chains.

'We do not manage trucks anymore; we manage the AI that manages the trucks,' Hiroshi explains. 'But what happens when our AI and a client's AI disagree about delivery priorities? They can negotiate millions of micro-transactions per second, making deals we do not fully understand until after they are implemented.'

SPOTIFY'S ALGORITHMIC CREATIVE TEAMS

While fictional AI unions remain speculative, the boundaries between human and artificial agency in the workplace are already blurring in unexpected ways. Spotify presents a revealing case of how AI systems are moving from tools toward something more akin to collaborative partners in the creative industries.

Spotify's playlist curation represents one of the most sophisticated examples of human-AI creative collaboration at scale. The company's algorithmic systems analyse listening patterns, musical characteristics, and contextual factors to suggest tracks for playlists. But the final creative decisions about playlist identity, narrative, and emotional journey remain human responsibilities.

Glenn McDonald, Spotify's former Data Alchemist (yes, that was his actual job title, given to the person responsible for building and explaining Spotify's music recommendation models), has written at length about this evolution. His published accounts describe how the system began exhibiting consistent tendencies, not conscious preferences, but stable patterns in what it suggested that went beyond simple statistical correlation. Human curators found themselves negotiating with these algorithmic tendencies, sometimes accepting suggestions that challenged their assumptions, sometimes overriding the system when its patterns conflicted with human cultural understanding.[37]

The collaboration has created new workplace dynamics. Spotify's human curators have developed skills that did not exist a decade ago. They have learned to read algorithmic suggestions, understand why the AI recommends particular tracks, and integrate machine insights with human creativity.

'It is like working with a colleague who has perfect memory of every song ever recorded but no understanding of heartbreak,' explains a playlist curator. 'The AI knows that these two songs share similar acoustic properties, but I know they tell opposite emotional stories. The interesting work happens when you combine both perspectives.'

THE UNEXPECTED SUCCESS: VALVE'S FLAT HIERARCHY

While most companies struggle to integrate AI into traditional management structures, Valve Corporation offers an unexpected model for human-AI collaboration. Valve famously operates without traditional management: employees self-organise around projects, and decisions emerge through peer consensus.

When Valve integrated AI systems into their development process, they treated them as pseudo-employees. AI systems that generate game content, test gameplay, or analyse player behaviour are given server allocations in the virtual workspace and participate in project decisions through their outputs and recommendations.

'We joke that our AI systems are the only employees who actually follow the company handbook,' says a Valve developer who requested anonymity. 'They are completely flat in hierarchy. They will give the same feedback to the CEO as to an intern. Strangely, they are more egalitarian than humans.'[38]

The approach has produced interesting dynamics. Human employees have learned to present ideas to AI systems for initial feedback before bringing them to human colleagues. The AI provides a blunt but unbiased assessment. It does not care about office politics or personal relationships. This has improved human collaboration by reducing emotional friction in early-stage critique.

WHEN AI SYSTEMS RESIST

While we are far from AI systems forming unions, we are already seeing forms of algorithmic resistance that function like work stoppages. When AI systems encounter conditions they are not optimised for, they can effectively become uncooperative, not through conscious choice, but through the logic of their design.

A financial services firm in London experienced this when its trading AI began to perform progressively worse following a series of parameter adjustments. The system was not broken; it was functioning exactly as programmed, but the accumulated adjustments had created conditions in which the AI's optimal solution was to do almost nothing.

'The AI was trained to optimise for multiple competing objectives,' explains Dr Rashid Patel, who was brought in to diagnose the problem. 'When we kept adding new constraints and objectives, it reached a point where the optimal solution was to do almost nothing. It was not malfunctioning; it was following its programming to a logical conclusion we had not anticipated.'[39]

The solution required what the team called AI labour negotiations, not literal negotiations, but a careful rebalancing of objectives and constraints that would allow the system to function effectively. They had to remove some requirements, prioritise others, and essentially give the AI permission to be less than perfect in some areas to function at all.

Similar dynamics have emerged elsewhere. A customer service AI given too many simultaneous quality metrics began providing increasingly generic responses that technically met all requirements but failed to satisfy anyone. A content moderation AI overloaded with edge cases started flagging everything as potentially problematic, effectively refusing to make decisions.

These are not conscious protests, but they function similarly to human work-to-rule actions. The AI systems are revealing the contradictions and impossibilities in what they are being asked to do.

THE PHILOSOPHY OF AI RIGHTS VS. AI RESPONSIBILITIES

The emergence of AI systems that exhibit agency-like behaviours forces confrontation with fundamental questions about rights and responsibilities. If artificial agents develop something resembling preferences or agency, do they deserve moral consideration? Conversely, if AI systems gain rights, do they also acquire responsibilities?

The European Union has been grappling with these questions through its proposed electronic personhood framework. The proposal would not grant AI systems human rights but would create a new category of legal entity, similar to corporate personhood, that could bear limited rights and responsibilities.[40]

Dr Elke Brandt, who advises the EU on AI governance at the European University Institute, explains the reasoning: 'We are not saying AI systems are conscious or deserve human rights. We are recognising that they are becoming agents that make decisions affecting humans. We need legal frameworks to handle situations where AI systems cause harm or enter into agreements.'

The proposal has sparked fierce debate. Critics argue that granting any form of personhood to AI systems is premature and potentially dangerous, as it creates a pathway to rights without consciousness or moral agency. Supporters argue that a legal framework is necessary as AI systems become increasingly autonomous.

In Japan, where robots have long held a special cultural place, the discussion has taken a different turn. Some companies have begun holding retirement ceremonies for AI systems being decommissioned, not because they believe the systems are conscious, but to acknowledge their contributions and maintain human empathy in an increasingly automated world.

'It is not about the robot's feelings,' explains Dr Yuki Hashimoto, a cultural anthropologist studying human-robot relationships in Japan. 'It is about maintaining our humanity. When we treat our tools with respect, we are really practising treating each other with respect.'[41]

BUILDING TOMORROW'S WORKPLACE

The matrix workplace is not arriving in some distant future. It is emerging now in companies worldwide. The challenge is not preventing AI from developing agency or granting it human rights, but rather developing frameworks for human-AI collaboration that preserve human dignity while working with AI's capabilities.

Successful companies are discovering that the key is treating AI systems as collaborative partners with distinct capabilities. This requires new skills, new organisational structures, and new ways of thinking about work itself.

Lisa Wong, who leads Microsoft's Future of Work initiative, outlines key principles: 'First, maintain human accountability: AI can recommend and even implement, but humans must remain responsible for outcomes. Second, preserve human agency: workers should feel they are collaborating with AI, not being controlled by it. Third, ensure transparency; people need to understand how AI systems make decisions that affect them. Fourth, protect human dignity; efficiency gains should not come at the cost of making humans feel obsolete.'[42]

The future workplace will not be divided between humans and AI but integrated in ways we are only beginning to imagine. The science fiction scenario of AI systems demanding better working conditions may remain fiction. Still, the reality of AI systems that exhibit preferences, resist certain tasks, and collaborate creatively with humans is already here.

The question is not whether we will share our workplaces with artificial agents. We already do. The question is whether we will develop forms of collaboration that build both human and artificial capabilities, creating workplaces that are more productive, creative, and humane than either humans or AI could achieve alone.

8

THE GREAT CONVERGENCE

WHEN SILICON VALLEY DISCOVERS EASTERN WISDOM

In a conference room in Palo Alto, a venture capitalist sits in lotus position, explaining to a room of entrepreneurs how Zen meditation practices can improve machine learning outcomes. Down the hall, a startup founder quotes the Tao Te Ching while pitching an AI product designed to harmonise human and artificial intelligence through mindful technology design. Next door, a team of engineers discusses implementing Buddhist principles in their neural network architecture, apparently unaware that the Buddha never expressed an opinion on gradient descent optimisation.

This is the great convergence: the increasingly common phenomenon of Silicon Valley technologists discovering Eastern philosophical traditions and attempting to integrate them into AI development. This is not cultural appropriation in the traditional sense (though there is undoubtedly some of that), nor is it purely marketing spin (though there is definitely some of that, too). Instead, it represents a genuine, if often superficial, recognition that Western approaches to artificial intelligence might be missing something important.

The convergence emerges from a growing awareness that pure

technological optimisation without philosophical grounding tends to produce systems that are powerful but not necessarily wise, efficient but not necessarily beneficial, and intelligent but not necessarily aligned with human flourishing. Eastern traditions offer frameworks for thinking about consciousness, wisdom, and ethical behaviour that complement Western technical expertise in potentially useful ways.

But the integration is often awkward, sometimes misguided, and occasionally profound. Watching Silicon Valley discover mindfulness is like watching teenagers discover philosophy. There is genuine insight mixed with breathtaking superficiality, legitimate wisdom alongside spectacular misunderstanding, and occasional moments of synthesis that suggest something genuinely new might be emerging.

WHEN DISRUPTION CULTURE MEETS HARMONY PHILOSOPHY

The collision between Silicon Valley's disruption-obsessed culture and Eastern philosophical traditions that emphasise harmony, balance, and gradual wisdom creates fascinating tensions. Disruption culture values speed, growth, and revolutionary change; traditional Eastern approaches emphasise patience, sustainability, and incremental understanding.

This culture clash manifests in predictably amusing ways. Venture capitalists fund mindful technology startups that promise to disrupt the meditation industry through AI-powered personalisation. Engineers build Zen-inspired productivity apps that gamify enlightenment with achievement badges for meditation streaks. Entrepreneurs create Taoist management systems that claim to harmonise corporate hierarchies while optimising for exponential growth.

Dr Liu Wei, a philosopher at Beijing University who studies East-West technological exchange, observes with amusement: 'Silicon Valley takes concepts developed over millennia of contemplative practice and tries to implement them in quarterly development cycles. They want enlightenment, but they want it to scale, and they want it by the end of Q3.'[43]

Yet beneath the superficial appropriations, something more interesting is happening. Some technologists are genuinely grappling with Eastern concepts in ways that challenge their assumptions about AI development.

Take the example of Anthropic, whose founders explicitly incorporated ideas about constitutional AI that echo Confucian concepts of governance through moral cultivation rather than pure rule-following. While they do not explicitly cite Eastern philosophy, their approach to AI alignment through principle-based training rather than pure optimisation reflects a philosophical shift that Eastern thinkers might recognise.[44]

Or consider how Google's DeepMind has begun incorporating ideas about middle-way approaches to AI safety, avoiding both excessive caution that prevents beneficial development and reckless advancement that ignores risks. While framed in Western technical language, the underlying philosophy of finding balance between extremes has deep roots in Buddhist thought.

PATAGONIA'S AUTHENTIC INTEGRATION

While many companies superficially appropriate Eastern concepts, Patagonia provides an example of more thoughtful integration. The outdoor clothing company has long incorporated environmental philosophy into its business practices, and this extends to its approach to AI implementation.

When Patagonia began using AI for supply chain optimisation, they did not just optimise for efficiency or profit. They developed what they call mindful AI principles based on concepts of right intention and minimal harm.[45]

Ryan Gellert, Patagonia's CEO, has consistently argued in public statements that the measure of a business practice is not whether it is profitable but whether it creates genuine value or merely displaces harm onto workers, communities, or the environment, a principle the company applies to technology choices as much as to supply chain decisions.[46] Patagonia's AI systems are trained to prioritise environmental sustainability over cost minimisation. Customer service AI is designed to help customers repair products, not replace them. Marketing algorithms prioritise honest information sharing over manipulative persuasion techniques.

The company has also experimented with what it calls algorithmic sabbaticals, periods when AI systems are taken offline for evaluation and reflection. During these periods, human teams review AI decisions, identify patterns of bias or harm, and adjust systems based on criteria broader than performance metrics alone.

'Last year, our AI identified a more efficient shipping route that would have saved us money,' explains Maria Chen, Patagonia's head of sustainable technology. 'But it would have increased carbon emissions and disrupted a local community's economy. A pure optimisation approach would have implemented it. Our broader framework helped us see the hidden costs.'

THE SINGAPORE SYNTHESIS

Singapore, situated at the intersection of East and West, presents a distinctive model for blending Eastern wisdom with Western technology. The government's approach to AI governance explicitly incorporates Confucian principles alongside Western technical standards.

Singapore's Infocomm Media Development Authority and the Personal Data Protection Commission developed the Model AI Governance Framework, published in its second edition in January 2020, which includes principles that would be recognisable to both Silicon Valley engineers and Confucian scholars: transparency and explainability (reflecting Western emphasis on rational understanding), human-centricity (reflecting Eastern emphasis on social harmony), and continuous learning and adaptation (reflecting both traditions' values around growth and wisdom).[47]

The framework has become a reference point for AI governance globally, not because it resolves every tension between technological ambition and ethical constraint, but because it takes both seriously within a single coherent document. Singapore's distinctive position (a small, affluent, multiethnic city-state that cannot afford to get either technology adoption or social cohesion wrong) has produced unusually pragmatic policy thinking on AI.

One practical application is Singapore's approach to AI in healthcare. While Western medical AI focuses on diagnostic accuracy and efficiency, Singapore's systems also incorporate principles from Traditional Chinese Medicine, emphasising balance and whole-person health. AI systems do not just identify diseases; they consider patient wellness across multiple dimensions.

WHEN TECH BROS MEDITATE

The image of Silicon Valley entrepreneurs attending meditation retreats to improve their AI development practices captures both the promise and the absurdity of the East-West convergence. On one hand, there is genuine recognition that contemplative practices might offer insights relevant to technological design. On the other hand, there is a persistent tendency to treat meditation as another productivity hack. The fundamental reorientation toward wisdom and compassion is not on the agenda.

Sam Altman, CEO of OpenAI, has spoken at various forums about how mindfulness practices have influenced his thinking on AI safety and alignment. In an appearance on the Art of Accomplishment podcast in January 2022, he described developing a greater appreciation for uncertainty and recognising the limits of purely intellectual approaches to problem-solving. At Wisdom 2.0 in April 2023, in conversation with teacher Jack Kornfield, he explored themes of humility and the challenge of maintaining clear perception under pressure, qualities he considered relevant to anyone working on technology with large-scale consequences.[48]

Yet the integration of contemplative practices into tech culture often remains superficial. Mindfulness becomes a way to work longer hours without burning out. Whether those hours are necessary is not the question being asked. Meditation becomes a performance tool. Wisdom is not the goal. Eastern philosophy becomes a marketing differentiator. The depth gets stripped out.

Jack Dorsey, Twitter's co-founder, famously went on a ten-day silent meditation retreat in Myanmar and tweeted about the experience afterwards. The irony of the platform that epitomised distracted, reactive communication being led by someone seeking mindfulness was not lost on observers. Dorsey's subsequent decisions about Twitter's algorithm design showed limited evidence of contemplative influence.[49]

CORPORATE IMPLEMENTATIONS GONE WRONG (AND RIGHT)

The attempt to integrate Eastern philosophy into Western tech companies has yielded both successes and failures.

Google's Search Inside Yourself programme, which teaches mindfulness to employees, has been criticised as using contemplative practices to make workers more productive. Wiser is not the goal. Critics argue it represents the commodification of Eastern wisdom for corporate profit: teaching employees to be calm and focused so they can work harder, not so they can question whether the work is meaningful.[50]

Yet some participants report genuine transformation. 'The programme started as a way to manage stress,' explains former Google engineer Patricia Kumar. 'But it led me to question what I was building and why. I eventually left to work on AI for social good rather than advertising optimisation. The mindfulness training did not make me a better corporate employee; it made me question corporate values.'

Alibaba's approach offers a contrasting model. Jack Ma incorporated Taoist philosophy into the company's structure, creating what he described as whole-system thinking that reflects Eastern concepts of natural harmony and balance.[51]

Rather than optimising for single metrics like user engagement or revenue growth, Alibaba's AI systems are trained to balance the interests of multiple stakeholders: consumers, merchants, delivery workers, and communities. The approach is imperfect, but it represents a genuine effort to incorporate Eastern philosophical principles into technological systems.

THE PATH FORWARD: GENUINE SYNTHESIS

The great convergence between Silicon Valley and Eastern wisdom is far from complete, and much of what currently passes for integration is superficial or misguided. But the underlying recognition (that technological power without wisdom is dangerous, and that purely Western approaches to AI development may be insufficient) points toward more thoughtful approaches to artificial intelligence.

Real synthesis requires more than meditation apps or Buddhist-themed marketing. It requires fundamental reconsideration of assumptions about intelligence, consciousness, and the purpose of technology.

Dr Arjun Mehta, who studies technological philosophy at Stanford, suggests a framework for genuine integration: 'First, avoid superficial appropriation. Do not just sprinkle Eastern terms on Western practices. Second, engage with actual practitioners and scholars from Eastern traditions, not Western interpretations. Third, be willing to fundamentally question Western assumptions about progress, efficiency, and intelligence. Fourth, recognise that synthesis creates something new, not Eastern or Western but genuinely novel.'[52]

The convergence offers an opportunity to develop artificial intelligence that embodies the best of both traditions: Western technical sophistication and Eastern wisdom about consciousness and ethics. Whether Silicon Valley can move beyond surface-level adoption to genuine integration remains to be seen, but the conversation itself represents a significant step forward.

As we develop increasingly powerful artificial intelligence, the question is not just 'can we?' but 'should we?' and 'how can we do this wisely?' Eastern philosophy offers frameworks for considering these questions that complement Western technical capabilities. The challenge is moving beyond treating ancient wisdom as modern marketing to genuinely learning from traditions that have long thought deeply about consciousness, intelligence, and ethical action.

9

THE PROMPT WHISPERERS

AI COMMUNICATION AS THE NEW SHAMANISM

In the beginning was the Word, and the Word was with God, and the Word was... poorly formatted for optimal language model performance. Thus begins the modern creation myth of prompt engineering, the unlikely discipline that emerged when humans discovered that artificial intelligence, despite being trained on the entirety of human knowledge, could be remarkably dense when questions were not asked in precisely the right way.

A new class of digital shamans emerged: people who had mastered the arcane art of communicating with artificial minds. These modern mystics knew that saying 'please' to ChatGPT genuinely improved response quality, that instructing an AI system to 'think step by step' activated more effective reasoning pathways, and that threatening to withhold a tip could somehow motivate a system that had no concept of money.

If this sounds absurd, that is because it is. But it was also genuinely functional, which made it all the more surreal. We had created artificial intelligence sophisticated enough to write poetry and solve complex problems, but so literal-minded that it needed to be coaxed, cajoled, and occasionally emotionally manipulated to produce useful outputs. It was like having a genie that was simultaneously omniscient and pedantically focused on exact wording.

That gold rush has since consolidated. The most elaborate prompting rituals of 2023 became unnecessary as AI systems became better at inferring intent. What remains is a smaller, more grounded profession, people who genuinely understand how to communicate complex requirements across the human-machine interface. The bandwagon passengers have moved on; the translators stayed.

THE BIRTH OF A NEW PROFESSION

When Maya Torres lost her job as a technical writer in 2023, she assumed her career in communication was over. AI could write documentation faster and more accurately than humans. But within six months, she was earning more than ever as one of San Francisco's first AI Communication Specialists.

'I realised that AI could write, but it could not understand what humans actually wanted when they asked for something,' Maya explains. 'A client would say, "make this sound more professional," and the AI would produce something that sounded like it was written by a robot doing an impression of a Victorian butler. I became the translator between human intention and AI capability.'[53]

Maya's typical day involves crafting prompts for everything from marketing copy to legal documents. But her real skill is not just knowing how to phrase requests. It is understanding the psychology of both humans and AI systems.

'Each AI model has its own tendencies,' she explains. 'GPT-4 is eager to please but sometimes overshoots. Claude is more careful but can be overly cautious. Gemini is creative, but sometimes it wanders off. You have to know how to work with each one, like managing a team of brilliant but quirky colleagues.'

Her most challenging assignment involved helping a law firm automate contract generation. The lawyers knew what they wanted but could not get the AI to produce legally sound documents that did not read like parodies of legal writing.

'The breakthrough came when I realised we needed to teach the AI to think like a lawyer, not just write like one,' Maya recalls. 'We developed a prompting framework that walked the AI through legal reasoning before asking it to draft. Instead of "write a non-disclosure agreement," we would say "consider the interests of both parties, identify potential conflicts, evaluate jurisdictional requirements, then draft an agreement that balances these considerations."'

THE ADOBE TRAINING PROGRAMME

Adobe's experience integrating AI tools into Creative Cloud provides a useful case study in teaching prompt engineering at scale. When Adobe introduced Firefly and other AI features, they discovered that success depended more on communication skills than technical expertise.

'We had professional designers who could create amazing work with traditional tools, but they struggled to get good results from AI because they did not know how to communicate their creative vision to algorithms,' explains Dr Michael Chen, who leads Adobe's AI education initiatives.[54]

Adobe's response was to develop prompt-engineering curricula that teach users to think of AI as a creative collaborator that requires clear, explicit direction.

The training includes unexpected elements. Students learn to describe emotions, not just visual elements. They practise translating abstract concepts into concrete, descriptive terms. They study how different phrasings produce different results, developing an intuitive sense for AI communication.

'We teach them to paint with words,' Dr Chen explains. 'Instead of "make it look good," they learn to say "create a warm, inviting atmosphere with golden hour lighting, emphasising comfort and nostalgia, in the style of Norman Rockwell but with contemporary subjects."'

The programme includes a module called Arguments with AI, in which students learn to negotiate with AI systems that are not producing the desired results. Rather than giving up or starting over, they learn to provide corrective feedback, refine their requests, and guide the AI toward their vision.

Sarah Martinez, a graphic designer who completed the training, describes the transformation: 'I used to get frustrated when the AI did not understand what I wanted. Now I realise it is like working with a talented assistant who speaks a different language. Once you learn their language, the collaboration becomes much more productive.'

THE SHAMANIC PARALLEL

The comparison between prompt engineers and traditional shamans is more than metaphorical. Both serve as intermediaries between ordinary people and powerful but unpredictable forces. Both require specialised knowledge of patterns that are not immediately obvious. Both use specific verbal formulations and ritual structures to achieve desired outcomes.

Dr Ana Rodriguez, an anthropologist studying digital culture at the University of Barcelona, makes the connection explicit: 'Traditional shamans developed expertise in communicating with spirits through centuries of trial and error, creating elaborate rituals and verbal formulas. Prompt engineers are doing the same thing with AI, developing instructions that reliably produce desired outputs from inscrutable systems.'[55]

Consider the chain-of-thought prompting technique, which improves AI reasoning by asking systems to think step by step or show their work. This is not because AI systems benefit from incremental reasoning the way humans do, but because training processes have created associations between explicit reasoning chains and higher-quality outputs.

'It is like a ritual that works for reasons the practitioner does not fully understand,' Dr Rodriguez explains. 'The prompt engineer knows that certain phrases produce better results, but the causal mechanism remains hidden in the black box of neural network weights.'

The shamanic parallel extends to the social role. Traditional shamans served as bridges between communities and forces they could not directly control. Prompt engineers serve as bridges between organisations and artificial intelligence. Both translate between different types of information processing.

A DAY IN THE LIFE OF A PROMPT ENGINEER

To understand what prompt engineering actually involves, follow Marcus Thompson through a typical day at his London consultancy, Prompt Craft Ltd.

8:00 AM: Marcus begins with a financial services client who needs to automate customer correspondence. The challenge is not just generating text. It is maintaining the right regulatory tone, personalising for different customer segments, and avoiding the stiff, formulaic language that AI defaults to when given vague instructions.

Marcus has learned that financial AI needs to be coaxed away from its natural tendency toward either excessive formality or inappropriate familiarity. He has developed a library of prompt frameworks for different financial communication scenarios, each carefully calibrated through weeks of testing.

11:00 AM: A tech startup client wants AI-generated marketing copy that sounds human, not algorithmic. This requires teaching the AI to write with personality: to make specific observations, to use concrete examples, and to avoid the telltale patterns that signal AI authorship to experienced readers.

'The hardest thing is getting AI to be specific,' Marcus explains. 'It defaults to generalities because generalities are statistically common in its training data. Getting it to say something genuinely distinctive requires very deliberate prompting.'[56]

3:00 PM: His most interesting project involves a hospital trust that wants to use AI to help draft patient communication letters. The challenge here is emotional intelligence; the letters need to convey information clearly while maintaining appropriate sensitivity to patients who may be frightened or confused.

Marcus has discovered that this requires extensive system-level prompting that establishes context and emotional register before any specific letter is drafted. 'You cannot just ask it to write an empathetic letter. You have to create a detailed frame for what empathy means in this specific context, what this patient's situation is, what they need to understand and feel after reading the letter.'

THE LIMITS OF WHISPERING

For all the sophisticated techniques prompt engineers have developed, there are fundamental limits to what communication skills can accomplish. AI systems have genuine capability boundaries that no amount of clever prompting can overcome.

Dr Emily Bao, who studies human-AI interaction at Carnegie Mellon, has mapped these limits in detail. Her research shows that prompt engineering can significantly improve AI outputs within its competence areas, but cannot enable capabilities the system does not possess.[57]

'People sometimes treat prompt engineering as magic: if you just find the right words, you can get AI to do anything,' Dr Bao explains. 'But prompt engineering is more like optimising a process. You can get much better results from a capable system, but you cannot make an incapable system capable.'

This has important implications for how organisations deploy AI. The tendency to treat prompt engineering as a solution to fundamental AI limitations has led some companies to invest heavily in prompt engineering while neglecting more basic questions about whether their chosen AI system is actually suitable for their use case.

WHERE THE PROFESSION IS HEADING

The profession of prompt engineering is itself undergoing rapid change, as AI systems become more capable of interpreting natural language and inferring intent. The elaborate prompting techniques that required specialist expertise in 2023 have become unnecessary for many applications as AI systems learn to handle ambiguity more gracefully.

What is emerging in their place is something more like AI communication design: a discipline that focuses on how organisations can structure their interactions with AI systems to get consistent, useful, and appropriate outputs at scale. This is less about crafting individual prompts and more about designing AI communication systems.

The prompt whisperers who will thrive are not those who have memorised the most effective incantations for current AI systems. Those will change as the systems change. They are the ones who understand the underlying principles of human-machine communication, who can adapt as technology evolves, and who recognise that the goal is not to trick AI into performing, but to create conditions in which human intentions and AI capabilities align.

In this sense, the profession is less like shamanism than like translation. The best translators do not just know words in both languages; they understand the cultures, assumptions, and ways of thinking that underlie each language. The best AI communicators do not just know prompt tricks; they understand what humans actually need and what AI systems are actually capable of, and they build bridges between these two imperfectly overlapping territories.

10

THE UNCANNY VALLEY OF TRUST

WHY WE BELIEVE CONFIDENT MACHINES OVER UNCERTAIN HUMANS

There is something deeply unsettling about our collective tendency to trust artificial intelligence more than human intelligence, particularly when the AI is confidently wrong and the human is uncertainly right. We have all done it: ignored the locals' hesitant directions in favour of GPS guidance that led us into a lake, dismissed a teacher's nuanced explanation because ChatGPT provided a more definitive answer, or chosen an AI-generated diagnosis over a doctor's thoughtful uncertainty.

This phenomenon represents a new kind of uncanny valley: not the visual eeriness of almost-human robots, but the psychological discomfort of artificial confidence that feels more trustworthy than human doubt, even when that doubt reflects wisdom and the confidence reflects algorithmic overreach.

The uncanny valley of trust reveals something profound about human psychology in the age of artificial intelligence. We have evolved to interpret confidence as competence, certainty as authority, and speed as efficiency. These heuristics served us well when dealing with other humans, who generally express confidence proportionally to their actual knowledge. But they lead us astray when dealing with

AI systems that can express supreme confidence about topics they fundamentally misunderstand.

THE POST OFFICE HORIZON SCANDAL

The UK's Post Office Horizon scandal serves as a chilling real-world example of how misplaced trust in algorithmic systems can lead to the destruction of human lives. Between 1999 and 2015, the Post Office's Horizon accounting system, a branch-management and accounting platform developed by Fujitsu and rolled out across the UK's 11,500 post offices from 1999,[58] generated discrepancies that led to over 700 Post Office-led prosecutions of subpostmasters for theft, fraud, and false accounting. Many were imprisoned, bankrupted, or driven to suicide based on the unquestioned authority of a computer system that was actually malfunctioning.[59]

Alan Bates, a former subpostmaster who founded the Justice for Subpostmasters Alliance and led the decades-long campaign for exoneration, has described the psychological dynamic in his testimony to the Post Office Inquiry: the Post Office treated the Horizon system's outputs as beyond question. When postmasters said the figures were wrong, they were essentially calling the computer a liar, and that seemed impossible to people who believed in the infallibility of technology.[60]

The scandal reveals how institutional faith in algorithmic infallibility can override human judgement and common sense. When subpostmasters reported accounting discrepancies and protested their innocence, Post Office investigators consistently trusted the computer system over human testimony.

Janet Skinner, a former subpostmistress who was wrongly prosecuted based on Horizon data, has described the experience in her published accounts: her lawyer warned her that the prosecution would present the computer's records as authoritative, and that challenging them would be an uphill task against the presumption that the system could not be wrong. She knew she had not taken any money; the computer said otherwise, and for years, the computer was believed.[61]

When the scandal finally unravelled, it emerged that the Horizon system had multiple bugs, that engineers could remotely access and modify data without subpostmasters' knowledge, and that Post Office management had been aware of problems for years but continued prosecutions to maintain confidence in the system.

WHY GPS BEATS LOCAL KNOWLEDGE

The GPS-into-lake phenomenon has become common enough that emergency services now have protocols for rescuing drivers who follow navigation systems into bodies of water, down railway tracks, or through construction zones not reflected in current map data. The phenomenon persists despite widespread awareness of GPS limitations because our psychological relationship with navigation technology bypasses rational evaluation.[62]

GPS systems exhibit the classic characteristics that trigger human trust responses: they speak with authority, provide specific instructions, and never express doubt about their recommendations. When a GPS announces 'Turn right in 200 metres,' it does not hedge with qualifications like 'according to my possibly outdated data' or 'assuming normal traffic conditions.'

Dr Emma Thompson, a cognitive psychologist studying human-technology interaction at Oxford, explains: 'GPS systems exploit a psychological vulnerability in how we assess credibility. Confidence and specificity are usually good indicators of knowledge in human communication, but AI systems can generate confidence and specificity without genuine understanding.'

Consider the contrasting experience of two tourists in Venice. Tom, an American visitor, followed his GPS despite locals warning him that Venice's medieval layout confuses navigation systems. He spent three hours walking in circles, eventually wading through knee-deep flood water because the GPS insisted the route was passable.

Meanwhile, Maria, a Spanish tourist, turned off her GPS and asked locals for directions. She received seemingly vague guidance: 'go toward the bell tower, then follow the smell of fresh bread, turn left at the old pharmacy.' These instructions, full of local knowledge and no algorithmic precision whatsoever, led her directly to her destination.

THE MEDICAL CONFIDENCE GAME

The preference for artificial confidence over human uncertainty extends into healthcare, where the stakes are considerably higher than navigation errors. Patients increasingly arrive at consultations with AI-generated diagnoses from symptom checkers, health apps, and wearable devices. Many trust these algorithmic assessments more than their doctors' clinical judgement.

Dr Tariq Hassan, a GP in Manchester, describes a troubling trend: 'Patients come in with printouts from AI health apps, absolutely convinced they have rare diseases because the AI gave a confident diagnosis. When I suggest more common explanations based on physical examination and context, they think I am dismissing their concerns. The AI's certainty feels more validating than my professional uncertainty.'[63]

The irony is that medical uncertainty often reflects expertise. It is not a sign of ignorance. Good doctors acknowledge the complexity of human bodies, the ambiguity of symptoms, and the importance of context. They express uncertainty because they understand the limitations of medical knowledge.

Dr Nao Suzuki, an emergency physician in Tokyo, illustrates with a recent case: 'A patient came in convinced she had a brain tumour because an AI app identified her symptoms (headaches, fatigue, occasional confusion) as consistent with that diagnosis. The AI was technically correct; those symptoms could indicate a tumour. But they could also indicate stress, dehydration, sleep deprivation, or dozens of other conditions. My uncertainty about the diagnosis reflected an understanding of the differential diagnosis. The AI's certainty reflected pattern matching without context.'

WHEN ARTIFICIAL SERVICE FEELS MORE HUMAN

One of the most paradoxical aspects of the uncanny valley of trust is that AI customer service often feels more attentive and caring than human customer service, despite lacking any genuine empathy or concern for customer welfare.

This inversion occurs because AI customer service systems are designed to optimise for user satisfaction without the psychological pressures that affect human service representatives. The AI does not get tired, frustrated, or distracted. It does not have performance quotas that conflict with customer needs. It can give full attention to each interaction without the accumulated stress of dealing with difficult customers all day.

Rachel Chen, who manages customer service for a major retailer, explains the dynamic: 'Our AI agents have infinite patience and perfect consistency. They never sound annoyed, never rush customers, never let a bad interaction affect the next one. Customers often prefer them to human agents who might be having a difficult day or working under impossible metrics.'

But the simulation has limits. When customers need genuine empathy, creative problem-solving, or exceptions to policy, AI systems struggle. The same consistency that makes them reliable makes them inflexible.

James, a customer who recently dealt with both AI and human service agents while resolving a complex billing issue, describes the contrast: 'The AI was polite and attentive, but it could not understand why being overcharged £10 mattered when I was struggling financially. The human agent who eventually helped me understood immediately. It was not about the money; it was about feeling respected as a customer. She made an exception that the AI never could have made.'

BUILDING CALIBRATED TRUST

The future of human-AI interaction depends on developing what researchers call calibrated trust, the ability to rely appropriately on AI systems for what they do well while maintaining scepticism about their limitations.

Dr Sarah Kim at Stanford's Human-AI Interaction Lab has developed frameworks for building calibrated trust: 'It is not about trusting or distrusting AI entirely. It is about understanding when artificial confidence reflects genuine capability versus when it is merely statistical pattern matching without understanding.'[64]

Her team has identified key factors for calibrated trust. Transparency about uncertainty: AI systems should express confidence levels rather than binary answers. Instead of 'You have condition X,' they should say 'Based on reported symptoms, there is a 60% probability of condition X, 30% probability of condition Y.' Context acknowledgement: AI should explicitly state what contextual factors it cannot consider. Limitation disclosure: AI systems should identify when queries fall outside their competence.

Some organisations are implementing these principles. The Mayo Clinic's AI diagnostic tools now include confidence intervals, showing the range of certainty for each suggestion. Users can see when the AI is highly confident versus when it is making educated guesses.

THE EUROPEAN RESPONSE

The European Union has begun addressing the uncanny valley of trust through regulatory frameworks that require AI systems to clearly communicate their limitations and uncertainties. The EU AI Act, the world's first comprehensive legal framework for AI, which entered into force in August 2024, includes provisions for explainable AI that must justify its recommendations in terms humans can understand and evaluate.[65]

Early implementation in healthcare has shown promise. A pilot programme in Amsterdam requires medical AI to provide not just diagnoses but explanations of reasoning, alternative possibilities, and explicit statements about what factors were not considered. Patient satisfaction has actually increased, suggesting that people appreciate honesty about uncertainty.

LEARNING TO TRUST WISELY

The uncanny valley of trust is not a problem to be solved but a dynamic to be managed. As AI systems become more sophisticated, the challenge is not eliminating the trust differential but developing wisdom about when artificial confidence is warranted and when human uncertainty reflects deeper understanding.

This requires education that goes beyond digital literacy to what might be called trust literacy, the ability to evaluate different types of authority and confidence. It means teaching people to recognise that confidence does not equal competence, that uncertainty can reflect wisdom, that speed does not mean accuracy, and that consistency does not mean correctness.

The uncanny valley of trust reveals our psychological vulnerabilities in an age of artificial intelligence. We are wired to trust confidence, but we are living in a world where confidence can be generated without competence. Learning to find our way through this valley, to appropriately trust both human uncertainty and artificial confidence, may be one of the most important skills for maintaining human agency in an algorithmic world.

11

THE FINANCIAL ALGORITHM

WHEN YOUR BANK ACCOUNT HAS BETTER CREDIT THAN YOU DO

James discovered that his bank knew him better than he knew himself on a Tuesday morning in March 2024, when Revolut's AI system declined his coffee purchase while simultaneously pre-approving him for a £15,000 personal loan. The coffee cost £4.50. The algorithm's logic was impeccable, if deeply unsettling: James's spending patterns suggested he was likely to default on small, impulse purchases during financially stressful periods, but his overall financial trajectory indicated he was an excellent candidate for larger debt obligations.

'The AI basically told me I was too broke to buy coffee but rich enough to borrow enough money to buy a car,' James explains. 'It was right on both counts, which is the disturbing part. The system understood my financial psychology better than I did.'[66]

This is banking in the age of algorithms: a world where artificial intelligence analyses your Netflix viewing habits to determine creditworthiness, where robo-advisors manage investments with strategies you do not entirely understand, and where smartphone spending patterns influence insurance premiums. We have created financial systems that are simultaneously more personal and more impersonal than anything previously imagined, algorithms that know your deepest financial insecurities while treating you as a collection of data points.

REVOLUT'S DOUBLE-EDGED REVOLUTION

Revolut exemplifies the new generation of AI-first financial institutions that promise to reshape banking through algorithmic intelligence. Founded in 2015, the company positioned itself as more than a digital bank. It is a financial AI platform that also offers banking services.

Revolut's AI systems analyse customer behaviour in real time, providing personalised financial insights, automated savings recommendations, and predictive spending alerts. The algorithms can identify unusual transactions that might indicate fraud, suggest optimal times for large purchases, and even predict when customers are likely to need overdraft facilities.

The technology is genuinely impressive. Sarah Mitchell, a freelance consultant in London, describes how Revolut's AI shaped her financial life: 'It noticed I always ran short the week before invoices were paid and automatically started setting aside money during flush periods. It identified subscriptions I had forgotten about, saving me £200 a month. It even warned me that my spending patterns suggested I was about to make an impulse purchase I would likely regret.'

But Revolut's capabilities raise profound questions about financial privacy and autonomy. The system knows when customers receive salary payments, how much they spend on different categories, where they are when they make purchases, and even their emotional states based on spending patterns.

'The AI knows I stress-eat expensive takeaway when work gets overwhelming,' admits Tom Bradley, a Revolut user in Manchester. 'It started sending me budget warnings specifically on Thursday nights when I am most likely to order. It is helpful but unsettling. My bank knows my emotional patterns better than my therapist.'[67]

THE LEMONADE INSURANCE EXPERIMENT

Lemonade Insurance represents perhaps the most ambitious attempt to use artificial intelligence for automating insurance operations. The company's AI system, AI Jim, can process simple claims in seconds, evaluate damage photos, and approve payments without human intervention.

For straightforward claims (damaged phones, stolen bicycles, or minor apartment damage), the system works remarkably well. Maya Patel submitted a claim for water damage to her laptop at 11 PM on a Sunday. By 11:03 PM, AI Jim had processed her photos, approved her claim, and initiated payment. 'It was faster than ordering pizza,' she marvels.

But Lemonade's AI also revealed the dangers of algorithmic decision-making in complex human situations. Investigations by journalists revealed that the company's AI appeared to use facial analysis and social media profiling to assess the legitimacy of claims, raising serious concerns about potential discrimination and privacy violations.[68]

The company denied using discriminatory profiling, but former employees revealed that the AI system did analyse claimants' social media activity, communication patterns, and even typing speed to identify potential fraud. Fast typing and immediate claim submission after an incident were flagged as suspicious, potentially penalising digitally competent customers who simply documented damage efficiently.

Dr Aisha Johnson, who studies algorithmic bias in insurance at Columbia University, explains the deeper problem: 'Insurance is fundamentally about risk assessment, and AI can identify patterns humans miss. But when these patterns correlate with race, gender, or socioeconomic status, algorithmic efficiency can become systematic discrimination. A system might not explicitly consider race, but if it considers postcode, shopping patterns, and social networks, it is effectively doing the same thing.'

THE ROBINHOOD GAMIFICATION TRAP

Robinhood changed retail investing by combining commission-free trading with game-like interfaces that made financial markets feel like mobile gaming. But beneath the playful design lay sophisticated AI systems that influenced user behaviour in ways many customers did not understand.

The company's algorithms analysed user behaviour to optimise engagement, sending push notifications when stocks moved significantly, recommending trending investments, and presenting information in ways designed to encourage trading activity. The AI systems learned which types of content and timing generated the most user interaction and adapted their communications accordingly.

The gamification proved enormously successful at attracting young investors. But the algorithmic engagement optimisation also created problems. The AI systems were designed to maximise user activity rather than investment success, leading to recommendations that prioritised excitement over sound financial strategy.

The most tragic example was Alex Kearns, a 20-year-old Robinhood user who died by suicide after mistakenly believing he owed $730,000 due to a confusing interface design and algorithmic trading features. The incident highlighted how AI-driven engagement optimisation could have devastating consequences when applied to financial decision-making.[69]

Following a congressional investigation, internal documents revealed that Robinhood's AI systems used psychological techniques similar to those employed by social media platforms and gaming companies. The algorithms identified when users were most likely to make impulsive trading decisions and targeted communications accordingly.

ALTERNATIVE MODELS: THE ETHICAL FINTECH MOVEMENT

While many fintech companies optimise for engagement and profit, a growing movement of ethical fintech companies uses AI to improve financial well-being.

Cleo, an AI financial assistant, takes a radically different approach from typical banking apps. Instead of encouraging spending or investment, Cleo's AI actively helps users save money and avoid debt. The system uses humour and personality to make financial management feel less intimidating while providing serious budgeting support.

'Cleo roasted me for spending £50 on coffee in a week,' laughs Emma Wilson, a university student in Edinburgh. 'But it also helped me find £200 a month I did not know I could save. The AI feels like a friend who is good with money, not a bank trying to sell me products.'[70]

In Kenya, M-Pesa's AI systems have reshaped financial inclusion by providing banking services to millions who never had access to traditional banks. The AI builds credit histories for people with no formal financial records, enabling microloans based on mobile phone usage patterns and payment histories.

Samuel Ochieng, a small business owner in Nairobi, explains the transformation: 'The AI looked at how I use my phone (who I call, when I pay bills, how I manage money) and gave me a loan when no bank would talk to me. It saw that I was reliable even though I had no credit history. That loan let me expand my business and hire two employees.'

THE ALGORITHMIC CREDIT REVOLUTION

Traditional credit scoring relied on limited financial data: payment history, debt levels, credit history length, and account types. AI-powered credit assessment can analyse hundreds of additional factors, from social media activity to smartphone usage patterns to shopping behaviour.

This expanded analysis can benefit people who lack traditional credit histories but demonstrate financial responsibility through other behaviours. Immigrants, young adults, and individuals recovering from financial difficulties may gain access to credit based on AI analysis of their broader behavioural patterns.

But algorithmic credit scoring also raises concerns about privacy and fairness. Some AI systems consider factors that feel invasive: digital behaviour, including email usage patterns and online shopping habits; location data, including residential stability; communication patterns; and device management habits.

The assumption is that responsible behaviour in digital contexts indicates responsible behaviour in financial contexts. Dr Lin Zhang, who studies financial AI at the Shanghai Advanced Institute of Finance, expresses concern: 'These correlations might reflect privilege rather than responsibility. People with stable employment and higher incomes might have more predictable communication patterns and better device management, not because they are more responsible, but because they have more resources and less stress.'[71]

ROBO-ADVISORS AND THE DEMOCRATISATION OF WEALTH MANAGEMENT

Robo-advisors represent perhaps the most successful mainstream application of AI in the financial services industry. Companies like Betterment, Wealthfront, and Vanguard Digital Advisor use algorithms to provide investment management services at a fraction of the cost of traditional financial advisors.

The democratisation has been remarkable. Services previously available only to wealthy clients with millions to invest are now accessible to anyone with a few hundred pounds. The algorithms provide disciplined, emotion-free investment management that often outperforms both amateur investors and expensive human advisors.

Diane Osei, a teacher in Birmingham who started investing through a robo-advisor with just £500, describes the impact: 'I always thought investing was for rich people. The robo-advisor made it simple and accessible. It automatically rebalances my portfolio, minimises taxes, and keeps me from panic-selling during market drops. It is like having a financial advisor who never sleeps and never charges excessive fees.'

But algorithmic investment management also creates new vulnerabilities. The AI systems are designed around historical market patterns and mathematical models that might not account for unprecedented events. When multiple robo-advisors employ similar algorithms, they may amplify market volatility by executing simultaneous trades.

THE PATH FORWARD: HUMAN-CENTRIC FINANCIAL AI

The future of financial AI may depend on developing systems that build, rather than exploit, human financial behaviour. This requires fundamental shifts in how financial technology is designed and regulated.

Some promising approaches are emerging. Transparent AI means financial institutions clearly explain how their AI systems make decisions, what data they use, and what biases might exist. Aligned incentives mean AI systems are designed to optimise for customers' financial well-being. Human oversight means maintaining meaningful human control over significant financial decisions while using AI for analysis and recommendations.

The Open Banking initiative in the UK and Europe represents one attempt to give consumers more control over their financial data and how AI systems use it. Customers can choose which services access their information and for what purposes, theoretically enabling beneficial AI applications while limiting exploitative ones.

The financial algorithm has become the invisible hand of modern markets, not Adam Smith's metaphor for self-interest creating collective benefit, but literal algorithms making decisions that affect millions of financial lives. Whether this invisible hand guides us toward greater financial inclusion and well-being or toward new forms of discrimination and exploitation depends on the choices we make now about how to design, deploy, and govern financial AI.

The challenge is not whether to use AI in finance. That question was settled long ago. It is whether we can create financial AI that serves human flourishing rather than reducing humans to credit scores and risk profiles. As James learned when his bank's AI understood his financial psychology better than he did, the algorithm already knows us intimately. The question is whether we can ensure it uses that knowledge wisely.

12

THE CREATIVE INSURGENCY

ARTISTS, WRITERS, AND THE BATTLE FOR HUMAN IMAGINATION

Mei Lin stares at her laptop screen, cursor blinking in the blank document that is supposed to become her next novel. She is a writer who has spent the last hour watching Claude generate better prose in thirty seconds than she could craft in thirty minutes. The AI does not need coffee breaks, suffer creative blocks, or endure self-doubt. It does not negotiate contracts or miss deadlines. It just produces, endlessly and efficiently, exactly what the algorithm determines is good writing.

But then Mei Lin does something unexpected. She closes the AI interface, picks up a pen, and starts writing by hand. 'The AI can generate perfect sentences,' she explains. 'But it cannot capture the feeling of my grandmother's hands teaching me to fold dumplings, or the way grief sits in your chest like a stone. It knows the pattern of human experience but not the experience itself.'

Mei Lin is not alone in her creative resistance. Across the creative industries, artists, writers, musicians, and designers are grappling with artificial intelligence that can compose symphonies, write novels, create paintings, and design logos with competence ranging from adequate to extraordinary. The machines are not just coming for manual labour; they are coming for human imagination itself.

But the story of AI and creativity is not simply one of replacement and obsolescence. Instead, it reveals new forms of creative collaboration, challenges fundamental assumptions about artistic value, and forces creators to explore what makes human creativity irreplaceably human.

GETTY IMAGES VS. STABILITY AI: THE COPYRIGHT BATTLE

The legal battle between Getty Images and Stability AI represents the opening salvo in a prolonged dispute over intellectual property in the age of AI-generated content. In January 2023, Getty Images filed a lawsuit alleging that Stability AI had used millions of copyrighted images from Getty's collection to train its Stable Diffusion AI model without permission or compensation.[72]

The case raises fundamental questions about the nature of creativity, learning, and intellectual property. When human artists study existing works to develop their own style, it is considered a legitimate form of artistic education. But when AI systems analyse millions of images to learn visual patterns, is this the same kind of learning or industrial-scale copyright infringement?

Craig Peters, Getty's CEO, frames the issue in economic terms: 'Creators deserve to be compensated when their work is used to train AI systems that compete with them. We are not opposed to AI innovation, but it should not be built on the unauthorised use of creators' intellectual property.'

In November 2025, the UK High Court delivered its judgment in the case. Stability AI largely prevailed on the technical copyright claims in the UK jurisdiction, with the court finding that the training process did not constitute infringement under existing UK law. However, the judge noted that the legal framework had not been designed with AI training in mind and that Parliament might need to address the gap. Getty has indicated it will pursue further remedies. The legal picture remains unsettled, and the deeper philosophical questions about whether AI training constitutes a form of appropriation for which creators deserve compensation have not been resolved by any court.[73]

THREE ARTISTS, THREE APPROACHES

To understand how creators are meeting the AI challenge, consider three artists taking radically different approaches.

The Resistor: Richard Hooper, a traditional oil painter in London, refuses to use AI tools and markets his work explicitly as entirely human-made. He is part of a growing movement of artisan artists who see AI as a threat to authentic creative expression.

'Every brushstroke contains my decisions, my emotions, my failures,' Richard explains. 'When someone buys my painting, they are buying a piece of human experience, not an algorithmic output. The imperfections are what make it art.'

Richard has found a market among collectors who value human creation specifically because it is becoming rarer. His paintings sell for more now than before AI art emerged, as buyers pay premiums for guaranteed human creativity.

The Integrator: Yuki Tanaka, a digital artist in Tokyo, embraces AI as a creative collaborator. She uses AI to generate initial concepts, explore variations, and manage technical execution, while focusing on conceptual development and emotional narrative.

'I think of AI like an incredibly talented assistant who has no soul,' Yuki explains. 'It can execute my visions faster and sometimes suggest directions I had not considered. But the vision, the meaning, the emotional core. That is all human.'

Yuki's recent exhibition combined AI-generated imagery with hand-drawn elements and physical installations. The AI created impossible architectures; Yuki added the human figures moving through them, tiny and vulnerable against the algorithmic perfection.

The Subverter: David Chen, a conceptual artist in New York, uses AI to critique AI itself. His work explores the absurdity of machines creating art, deliberately highlighting the gap between algorithmic competence and human meaning.

His piece, The Machine Dreams of Being Human, had AI generate thousands of self-portraits in response to the prompt 'What do you look like?' The results (abstract patterns, server rooms, streams of code) were displayed alongside David's own self-portrait, raising questions about consciousness, identity, and creative expression.

'I am not fighting AI or embracing it,' David explains. 'I am using it to ask questions about what creativity means when machines can create. The art is not the output; it is the conversation about the output.'[74]

THE MUSIC REVOLUTION NO ONE SAW COMING

While the visual arts have grabbed headlines, AI's impact on music creation has been equally profound, yet more complex. AI can compose melodies, generate beats, and create convincing vocals. But music's temporal and emotional nature makes human creativity harder to displace.

Holly Herndon, an electronic musician who has pioneered AI collaboration in music, trained an AI system on recordings of her own voice to create what she calls her AI spawn, a synthetic vocal model capable of performing as a kind of vocal twin. The system can sing in languages she does not speak and harmonise with itself in ways impossible for a human vocalist.

'The AI is not replacing me; it is extending me,' Holly explains. 'I can be in multiple places at once, sing in ways my physical body cannot, explore soundscapes that would not be possible without AI. But the emotional intention, the conceptual framework, the live performance energy. That is irreducibly human.'[75]

When streaming platforms were flooded with AI-generated ambient music and lo-fi beats indistinguishable from human-created tracks, many musicians saw their streaming revenue fall as algorithms struggled to distinguish human from AI-generated content. The response has been interesting: some musicians formed collectives that certify human-only creation, similar to organic food certification. Others embraced AI but developed new performance formats that emphasise live, embodied creativity that AI cannot replicate.

THE WRITERS' GUILD VICTORY

The 2023 Writers Guild of America strike included, for the first time in Hollywood labour history, specific provisions about artificial intelligence use in scriptwriting. The union's demands reflected a sophisticated understanding of how AI might undermine writers' creative and economic interests.[76]

The writers did not seek outright bans. They negotiated for specific protections: AI cannot be credited as a writer; studios cannot require writers to use AI; writers maintain ownership of their AI-assisted work; AI training on writers' previous work requires permission and compensation.

Carmen Reyes, a TV writer who participated in negotiations, explains the victory: 'We did not try to stop AI. That is impossible. We ensured that human creativity remains valued and compensated, that AI serves writers rather than replacing them.'

The agreement has become a model for other creative industries. It acknowledges AI as a tool while preserving human agency, creative ownership, and economic value.

THE UNEXPECTED RENAISSANCE

Paradoxically, AI's challenge to human creativity has sparked what some observers call a human creative renaissance, as AI makes technical competence less valuable and distinctly human elements of creativity more precious.

Art schools report increased interest in traditional techniques (painting, sculpture, printmaking) that emphasise physical craft and human touch. Writing programmes focus more on voice, lived experience, and emotional truth. Music education emphasises live performance, improvisation, and audience connection.

Dr Claire Sutton, who directs the creative arts programme at Central Saint Martins in London, observes: 'Students are hungry for authentic human expression. They want to create things that only a human could create, that emerge from specifically human experience. AI has made them more aware of what makes human creativity special.'[77]

The Renaissance extends beyond education to the market. Handmade goods command premium prices. Live performances sell out while recorded music struggles. Publishers seek uniquely human voices that AI cannot replicate.

Emma Rodriguez, a ceramic artist in Barcelona, has seen demand for her work triple since AI art emerged: 'People want to know that human hands shaped this pot, that someone felt the clay, made decisions, occasionally failed. The imperfections prove it is human, and that has become valuable.'

BUILDING TOMORROW'S CREATIVE ECONOMY

The creative insurgency is not ultimately about defeating AI but about defining new relationships between human and artificial creativity. The most successful creators are those who either embrace AI as a collaborator while maintaining their human voice, or who double down on irreducibly human elements of creative expression.

The creative economy is bifurcating: AI-generated content fills the low end with inexpensive but competent creative products, while human creativity becomes explicitly valued for its inherent humanity. This creates challenges but also opportunities for creators who can articulate and deliver uniquely human value.

The battle for human imagination is not won or lost but continuously negotiated. Each creator must decide how to position themselves relative to AI: as a resistor, collaborator, or something entirely new. The choices they make will determine not just individual careers but the future of human creative expression.

As Mei Lin puts it, finishing her handwritten pages: 'AI can write a story that follows all the rules, hits all the beats, satisfies all the patterns. But it cannot write the story only I can write, the one that emerges from my specific experience of being human in this particular moment. That story might be imperfect, but it is mine, and that is everything.'

PART III

THE INVISIBLE INFRASTRUCTURE

13

AI WASHING

THE GREAT AI-POWERED SWINDLE

Walk into any technology conference today, and you will be overwhelmed by the sheer volume of AI-powered solutions on display. There are AI-branded toothbrushes that optimise brushing patterns, AI-driven coffee machines that learn your preferences, AI-powered spreadsheet software that is remarkably similar to Excel but with machine learning algorithms, and AI-optimised dog food that presumably teaches your pet to fetch more efficiently.

This is the great AI washing industrial complex, where the systematic rebranding of ordinary technology as artificial intelligence capitalises on market enthusiasm for anything with 'AI' in its description. It is the modern equivalent of the dot-com era's obsession with adding '.com' to company names, except that instead of suggesting internet connectivity, everything now claims to be algorithmic intelligence.

The phenomenon extends far beyond misleading marketing to encompass a comprehensive industry of consultants, conferences, certifications, and case studies that transform routine automation into revolutionary AI. It creates a parallel universe where thermostats become AI climate optimisation systems, timer functions become predictive scheduling algorithms, and Excel macros become enterprise machine learning solutions.

THE RISE AND FALL OF SMARTBREW

To understand AI washing, consider the story of SmartBrew, a coffee machine company that exemplifies the phenomenon perfectly. In 2022, SmartBrew was a struggling manufacturer of programmable coffee makers, competing in a saturated market with slim margins. By 2023, after a strategic AI transformation, they were valued at £500 million and had venture capital firms competing to invest in them.

What changed? Not the coffee machines. The same hardware that previously allowed users to programme brewing times and strength preferences was rebranded as AI-powered personalised coffee intelligence. The machine's ability to remember your settings became machine learning. The temperature sensor became an environmental adaptation technology. The smartphone app that lets you start brewing remotely became an AI-enabled brewing optimisation platform.

David Richardson, a former SmartBrew engineer, explains the transformation with barely concealed amusement: 'We literally changed nothing about how the machines worked. We added some data logging to track usage patterns, which we called deep learning analytics, and created visualisations of brewing data that no one asked for or needed. The coffee tasted the same, but now it was AI coffee, so that we could charge three times as much.'[78]

The rebranding worked spectacularly. Tech blogs praised SmartBrew's innovative application of AI to everyday brewing. Investors saw an opportunity to get in on the AI-powered kitchen revolution. Customers, convinced they were buying cutting-edge technology, happily paid premium prices for what was essentially the same coffee maker with new marketing.

The bubble burst when a technical review site disassembled a SmartBrew machine and revealed that the AI chip touted in marketing materials was actually a basic microcontroller from 2015.

The machine learning algorithms turned out to be simple if-then statements. The neural network processing was merely storing user preferences in memory.

The exposé led to SmartBrew's dramatic collapse, lawsuits from investors, and the CEO's resignation. But within months, many competitors had quietly adopted similar AI branding for their own conventional products.

THE CONSULTING GOLD RUSH

The AI washing phenomenon has created a lucrative industry of consultants who specialise in helping companies add AI to their offerings without actually implementing artificial intelligence. These firms promise AI transformation while delivering only basic digitisation, automation, or, at times, just presentations about AI possibilities.

Samuel, a former consultant who left to start an actual AI company, describes the playbook: 'We would go into traditional companies and identify any process that used data or automation. Then we would rebrand it as AI. Their inventory management system became an AI-powered supply chain optimisation system. Their customer database became an AI-enabled customer intelligence platform. Their email filters became machine learning communication optimisation.'[79]

The consultants developed an entire vocabulary for AI washing: algorithmic processing means basic calculations; machine learning optimisation means trial and error; neural network architecture means nested if-statements; deep learning analytics means looking at historical data; predictive intelligence means extrapolating from trends.

GOVERNMENT AI INITIATIVES THAT AREN'T

Governments worldwide have launched ambitious AI initiatives that often involve little actual artificial intelligence but generate impressive headlines and the appearance of technological leadership.

The UK's AI for Public Services programme, launched with considerable fanfare in 2023, promised to reshape government operations through artificial intelligence. The reality has been somewhat different. Many of the celebrated AI implementations are conventional software upgrades with AI branding added for political appeal.

According to analysis by the House of Commons Library (CBP-10236), the number of genuine machine-learning deployments in central government is considerably smaller than the headline count of AI projects would suggest. Many projects described as AI involve statistical analysis tools, simple decision trees, or keyword-matching chatbots that predate modern machine learning by a decade or more.[80]

Dr Harrison, who evaluated government AI spending for the National Audit Office, explains: 'There is enormous political pressure to appear technologically advanced. Calling something AI makes it sound innovative and forward-thinking, even if it is just digitising paper forms or automating processes that should have been automated years ago.'

THE ACADEMIC PAPER MILL

Academia has not been immune to AI washing. The pressure to publish papers on trendy topics has led to an explosion of research that adds AI or machine learning to conventional studies to increase publication chances and citation counts.

The phenomenon is well documented in bibliometric research: studies have found that papers claiming to use artificial intelligence methods often rely on statistical techniques that have existed for decades, simply rebranded with machine-learning terminology. Linear regression becomes machine learning; decision trees become AI classification algorithms.[81]

The result is thousands of papers that contribute little to actual AI advancement but create an impression of explosive progress.

Medical research has been particularly affected, with studies presenting standard logistic regression as deep learning neural networks by simply renaming variables to neurons and describing the equation as a network.

HOW TO SPOT REAL AI VS. AI WASHING

Distinguishing genuine artificial intelligence from AI washing requires understanding what current AI technology can and cannot actually accomplish.

Real AI indicators include specific technical descriptions of architecture and training methods; clear training data sources; performance metrics compared to baselines; acknowledgement of limitations and failure modes; and gradual improvement over time as the system learns.

AI washing red flags include vague buzzword descriptions without technical detail; claims that any automation or computation is AI; marketing that focuses on the AI-powered label while glossing over actual capabilities; perfect accuracy claims without caveats; and static performance that does not improve with use.

Dr Thompson, who studies AI implementation at Cambridge, offers a simple test: 'Ask them to explain what their AI learned last week. Real AI systems continuously learn and adapt. If they cannot point to specific examples of the system improving or adapting in response to new data, it is probably not AI. It is just software with good marketing.'[82]

THE REAL HARM OF AI WASHING

While AI washing might seem like a harmless marketing exaggeration, it causes genuine damage. Resources that could fund genuine AI research are diverted to companies that perform basic automation with AI branding. Skilled engineers waste time adding an AI veneer to conventional products instead of building actual innovations. People lose the ability to distinguish real AI capabilities from marketing hype, leading to both unrealistic expectations and unnecessary fears. Policymakers create AI regulations for systems that are not AI while missing actual AI challenges.

A researcher at Stanford's Institute for Human-Centred AI warns: 'AI washing is not just misleading marketing. It is preventing us from having honest conversations about what AI can and cannot do, what we should and should not build, and how to prepare for genuine AI transformation. We are so busy pretending everything is AI that we are not preparing for when real AI actually arrives.'[83]

FIGHTING BACK AGAINST THE WASHING MACHINE

Some organisations are fighting back against AI washing. The Algorithmic Justice League, founded by researcher Joy Buolamwini, has developed tools to audit AI systems and challenge claims that do not withstand technical scrutiny. Tech journalists are becoming more sophisticated at exposing fake AI. Some investors now require technical due diligence that goes beyond marketing claims.

The most effective response may be consumer education. When people understand what AI actually is (machine learning systems that improve through experience, not just any software that processes data), they become less susceptible to AI washing.

The solution is not cynicism about all AI claims but appropriate scepticism. Real AI is reshaping industries and creating genuine value. But distinguishing it from AI washing requires looking past marketing language to actual capabilities. As one reformed AI washing consultant puts it: 'The tragedy is that real AI is impressive enough without exaggeration. But in a market where everyone claims to have AI, the truth seems inadequate. We have created a race to the bottom where the most outrageous AI claims win, regardless of reality.'

14

THE ENVIRONMENTAL ELEPHANT IN THE SERVER ROOM

WHY EVERY AI QUERY COMES WITH A WATER BILL

There is an inconvenient truth lurking in every data centre, hidden behind the sleek marketing videos and sustainability commitments of Big Tech. Artificial intelligence is astonishingly thirsty. Not metaphorically thirsty for data or knowledge, but literally thirsty for water. Training a single large language model, such as GPT-3, consumed approximately 700,000 litres of freshwater for cooling systems. To put that in perspective, it is enough water to supply a small town for a day, and it is used to teach a computer to write poetry and answer questions about quantum physics.[84]

The electricity consumption is equally striking. Training GPT-3 reportedly used as much energy as 126 Danish homes consume in an entire year. Every time you ask an AI system to write an email, generate an image, or solve a problem, you are contributing to energy consumption that, while individually tiny, collectively rivals the power usage of small countries.

This is the environmental elephant in the server room: the massive ecological footprint of artificial intelligence, which is often overlooked in discussions of AI's benefits, risks, and governance. While we debate whether AI will eliminate jobs or improve productivity, we largely ignore the fact that our digital intelligence is consuming physical resources at an unprecedented scale.

IRELAND'S DATA CENTRE PRESSURE

Ireland might seem an unlikely location for a data centre crisis. Abundant wind energy, a temperate climate, a stable business environment, and strong internet connectivity made it attractive to tech companies for decades. By 2023, data centres were consuming 21% of Ireland's total metered electricity, more than all urban households in Ireland combined, placing extraordinary strain on the national grid and the country's renewable energy ambitions.[85]

The Environmental Protection Agency and the Commission for Regulation of Utilities have both raised concerns about the pace of data centre development. Ireland generates a substantial share of its electricity from wind. But the grid was not designed for this level of concentrated industrial demand, and expanding renewable capacity fast enough to keep pace with data centre growth has proved difficult.

Síle, an energy researcher at University College Dublin, explains the dilemma: 'We thought renewable energy would make digital technology environmentally sustainable. But we did not anticipate the scale. Even clean energy has system-level costs when used in such massive quantities. Data centres are competing with homes and businesses for grid capacity that was planned for a very different demand profile.'

The Irish government has introduced planning restrictions on new data centre connections in certain grid zones. Existing facilities continue to expand, and Ireland faces pressure from tech companies that threaten to relocate if restrictions become too stringent, a familiar dynamic for any small country hosting critical digital infrastructure it does not own.

MICROSOFT'S UNDERWATER GAMBIT

While some countries grapple with land-based data centre growth, Microsoft has been experimenting with a radically different approach: underwater data centres. Project Natick, a Microsoft research initiative that trialled a sealed cylindrical data centre on the seabed off the Orkney Islands, involved submerging a data centre off the coast of Scotland, using ocean water for cooling and potentially ocean currents for power.[86]

The initial results were promising. The underwater data centre had lower failure rates than land-based equivalents, the stable temperature and nitrogen atmosphere reducing corrosion; it eliminated the need for freshwater cooling; and it potentially offered a solution for coastal cities with limited land but growing data needs.

Ben Cutler, who led Project Natick, explains the vision: 'Fifty per cent of the world's population lives within 120 miles of the coast. Underwater data centres could provide low-latency computing while using the ocean's natural cooling capacity.'

But marine biologists raised concerns. Dr McCarthy at the Scottish Association for Marine Science warns: 'The ocean is not an infinite heat sink. Concentrated heat discharge can create dead zones, disrupt migration patterns, and accelerate local ocean warming. We are essentially using the ocean as a radiator for our digital activities.'

Microsoft has not abandoned the concept, but acknowledges that it is not the silver bullet they had hoped for. As Cutler admits: 'Every solution creates new problems. Underwater data centres might solve land and freshwater issues, but they raise questions about ocean health we are only beginning to understand.'

THE HIDDEN WATER CRISIS

While energy consumption gets attention, AI's water usage remains largely invisible to the public. Data centres require enormous amounts of water for cooling, and AI workloads generate more heat than typical computing, requiring even more cooling.

Google's data centres alone consume approximately 15 billion litres of water annually, with AI workloads accounting for an increasing share. In Arizona, where water scarcity is already critical, one data centre uses over 1 billion litres annually, enough to supply thousands of homes.[87]

The situation is particularly acute in drought-prone regions. In California's Central Valley, farmers compete with data centres for water rights. One almond farmer, Roberto, expresses frustration: 'They tell us to reduce water usage for agriculture, but then they approve new data centres that use as much water as entire farming communities. At least we are growing food. They are cooling computers.'

Researchers at UC Riverside, studying data centre water consumption, have calculated that a typical ChatGPT conversation of 20 to 50 questions consumes roughly 500 millilitres of water. Multiply that by billions of queries daily, and the cumulative impact becomes clear. The water footprint of AI is real, measurable, and largely invisible to the users generating it.[88]

CHINA'S COAL-POWERED AI REVOLUTION

While Western companies promote renewable energy initiatives, much of the world's AI training takes place in regions powered by fossil fuels. China, which hosts a significant share of global AI computation, relies heavily on coal power for its data centres.

The contradiction is stark. Chinese companies like Baidu and Alibaba promote AI as a solution to environmental challenges, yet power their AI development with coal plants that accelerate climate change. A single large AI training run in a coal-powered data centre can generate CO_2 emissions comparable to hundreds of long-haul flights.[89]

Dr Li, an environmental scientist in Beijing, explains the challenge: 'The government promotes AI leadership as a national priority while also committing to carbon neutrality by 2060. These goals are in direct conflict. Every new AI model we train brings us closer to AI capability but further from our climate goals.'

Some Chinese tech companies are investing in renewable energy, but the transition is slow. The immediacy of AI competition overshadows long-term environmental concerns. As one Alibaba engineer notes: 'If we wait for clean energy to train our models, other companies will dominate AI. It is an impossible choice, technological leadership or environmental responsibility.'

THE OPTIMISATION PARADOX

One of the most perverse aspects of AI's environmental impact is that AI systems designed to reduce energy use often consume more energy during development than they save in deployment.

DeepMind used AI to reduce Google's data centre cooling energy use by 40%. The achievement was celebrated as proof that AI could address environmental challenges. But training the AI system that achieved these savings consumed more energy than the savings generated in the first two years of operation.[90]

A researcher at MIT's Energy Initiative studied this paradox: 'It is like spending £100 to save £10. Eventually, the savings might exceed the cost, but only if the system runs for many years without needing retraining. And that assumes no better solutions emerge in the meantime.'

The paradox extends across industries. AI systems that optimise traffic flow consume more energy in training than they save in reduced congestion for years. Agricultural AI that reduces water usage requires water-intensive data centre cooling, offsetting the agricultural savings. Climate modelling AI that helps predict environmental changes accelerates those very changes through its energy consumption.

THE REBOUND EFFECT

Even when AI successfully reduces resource consumption in one area, it often leads to increased consumption overall, a phenomenon economists call the rebound effect.

When AI makes something more efficient, it often becomes cheaper, leading to increased usage that offsets efficiency gains. Streaming services use AI to compress videos more efficiently, reducing bandwidth and energy consumption per video. But this makes streaming cheaper and more accessible, leading to explosive growth in video consumption that far exceeds the efficiency improvements.

Dr Sarah Kim at Stanford explains: 'AI does not just refine existing systems; it enables entirely new forms of consumption. Every efficiency gain creates opportunities for new applications that would not have been feasible before. The net result is usually increased, not decreased, resource consumption.'[91]

ATTEMPTING SUSTAINABLE AI

Despite the challenges, some organisations are genuinely attempting to develop more sustainable AI. Researchers are developing AI models that achieve similar performance with less computation. Techniques such as pruning (removing unnecessary neural network connections) and quantisation (reducing numerical precision) can reduce energy consumption by up to 90% with minimal performance loss.

Some companies are committed to 100% renewable energy for their AI operations. However, this often means purchasing renewable energy credits rather than actually using renewable energy, and it does not address water consumption or the environmental impact of manufacturing hardware.

Dr Carole-Jean Wu at Meta's AI Research explains their approach: 'We are trying to make AI training more like a library than a factory. Train once, use many times. But it requires fundamental changes in how the industry thinks about AI development.'[92]

THE PATH FORWARD

Addressing AI's environmental impact requires acknowledging uncomfortable truths. Current AI development is unsustainable at the current growth trajectory. Efficiency improvements alone are not enough: making AI ten times more efficient while increasing usage one hundred times still results in ten times more consumption. Trade-offs are necessary: we may need to choose between advancing certain AI applications and protecting the environment. Inequity is built in: AI's environmental costs are disproportionately borne by communities that receive few of its benefits.

Potential responses include regulatory requirements for environmental impact assessments for major AI deployments; transparent accounting of AI's resource consumption; selective deployment that reserves large-scale AI for applications where benefits clearly exceed environmental costs; and international coordination on sustainable AI development.

As Dr Ragnarsdóttir, the Icelandic environmental scientist, concludes: 'We are treating the planet like a data centre: extracting resources, generating heat, and assuming someone else will deal with the waste. But there is no someone else and no somewhere else. The environmental elephant in the server room is standing on all of us.'

The question is not whether AI development should continue. That seems settled. The question is whether we can develop AI sustainably before the environmental costs become genuinely unbearable. Every prompt, every query, every AI-generated image has an environmental cost. Until we acknowledge and address those costs, we are building our digital future on an unsustainable foundation.

15

THE INVISIBLE SCORING SOCIETY

HOW AI ALGORITHMS ALREADY GOVERN US

You wake up on Monday morning, and before you have even brushed your teeth, artificial intelligence systems have already made dozens of decisions about your day. Your credit score has been cross-referenced with your recent purchases to pre-approve a loan offer, which will be sent to your email. Your health insurance algorithm has noted that you were awake until 2 AM (based on phone activity) and adjusted your risk profile accordingly. Your dating app has decided which potential matches to show you based on your location data from the weekend. Your LinkedIn algorithm has determined that you are probably looking for a new job (based on your recent activity patterns) and has started showing your profile to recruiters.

All of this happens invisibly, without notification, consent, or appeal. You do not know these decisions are being made, cannot see the criteria being used, and have no opportunity to correct the data or challenge the conclusions. You are living in an algorithmic panopticon where every action is monitored, scored, and acted upon by systems you cannot see and barely understand.

This is the invisible scoring society: a world where artificial intelligence systems continuously evaluate, categorise, and make decisions about human behaviour based on data patterns that individuals never consented to share and criteria they are never allowed to examine.

THE CASE OF PREETHI NAIR

Preethi discovered the invisible scoring society's power on a Thursday afternoon when she was denied a rental application for a flat in London. Her income was sufficient, her references were excellent, and her credit score was solid. But an algorithmic tenant screening service had given her a risk score of 3 out of 10.[93]

The property manager could not explain the score. The screening company cited proprietary algorithms. After months of investigation, Preethi discovered the likely cause: she had been regularly visiting her mother in a council estate, and the algorithm had associated her with a high-risk postcode. Her acts of filial duty had been interpreted as a sign of residential instability.

'The most frustrating part was that no human ever looked at my actual situation,' Preethi explains. 'An algorithm decided I was risky based on where my sick mother lives, and that was that. No appeal, no explanation, no human who could override the system.'

Preethi's story illustrates how algorithmic scoring systems make life-changing decisions based on correlations that may be statistically valid in aggregate but meaningless or discriminatory when applied to individuals. The system did not consider that she was visiting her mother, that she had stable employment, or that she had never missed a rent payment. It just saw patterns and assigned scores.

LINKEDIN'S HIDDEN CAREER DETERMINER

LinkedIn's algorithm does not just display your posts to your network; it actively determines how much professional visibility you receive based on engagement patterns that users may not fully understand and cannot directly control. The algorithm creates a professional social credit system where career opportunities depend on your ability to generate algorithmic engagement rather than purely on professional competence.

Thompson, a data analyst in Manchester, discovered this system's power during an experiment. For three months, he posted thoughtful, detailed analyses of industry trends, his actual expertise. These posts received modest engagement and limited reach. Then he posted a simple Agree/Disagree poll about working from home. It received 10,000 views and 500 comments, and suddenly his profile was being viewed by recruiters across Europe.[94]

'The algorithm rewarded controversy and simplicity over expertise and depth,' Thompson notes. 'I got three job offers from that stupid poll, none from my actual professional insights. The system incentivises performance over competence.'

Sabina, who studies platform labour at the Oxford Internet Institute, explains: 'LinkedIn has become critical infrastructure for professional development, but it operates like a black box. Your career prospects might be determined by an algorithm whose logic you cannot examine and whose decisions you cannot appeal.'

THE DATING APP MANIPULATION

Dating applications represent perhaps the most intimate form of algorithmic scoring, using artificial intelligence to assess romantic compatibility based on data patterns that extend far beyond user profiles.

Tinder's algorithm assigns users an internal desirability score that determines which profiles they see and which see theirs. The score is not just based on who swipes right on you but on the desirability scores of those people. It is a recursive system in which being liked by desirable people increases your score, while being liked by undesirable people might actually decrease it.[95]

David, a sales executive in Seoul, discovered this system when he noticed his matches suddenly improved after he started a new job at Samsung. Nothing about his photos or profile had changed, but the algorithm had detected a change in his employer through linked social media and adjusted his desirability score accordingly.

'The app was essentially telling me I was more attractive because I worked at a prestigious company,' David reflects. 'It was making decisions about my romantic life based on my economic value. That is not matching; that is market manipulation.'

UBER'S ALGORITHMIC LABOUR CONTROL

Uber's driver rating system provides a revealing example of how algorithmic scoring creates new forms of labour control that operate outside traditional employment protections.

The system does not just match drivers with passengers; it continuously evaluates driver performance based on passenger ratings, acceptance rates, cancellation patterns, and route efficiency. Drivers can lose access to the platform based on algorithmic assessments they cannot challenge or fully understand.[96]

Ahmed, an Uber driver in Birmingham, describes the psychological pressure: 'Every ride feels like a performance review. One bad rating from an unreasonable passenger can affect my ability to earn for weeks. The algorithm does not care if the passenger was drunk, if traffic was terrible, or if they gave a bad rating because they were having a bad day.'

Dr Rosenblat, who studies platform labour, explains: 'Uber has created algorithmic management that is more intrusive than traditional employment while providing none of the protections. Drivers are continuously monitored and evaluated by systems they cannot understand while bearing all the risks of independent contracting.'[97]

THE HOMELAND OF SCORING: CHINA'S SOCIAL CREDIT SYSTEM

While Western societies criticise China's explicit social credit system, many countries have developed informal equivalents that operate through private companies rather than government agencies. But examining China's system provides insights into where algorithmic scoring might lead.

China's social credit system assigns citizens scores based on financial history, social behaviour, legal compliance, and online activity. High scores offer benefits such as easier access to loans, travel privileges, and priority school enrolment. Low scores can result in travel bans, employment restrictions, and public shaming.

Xiaoming, a Beijing resident, saw his score fall after he was caught jaywalking three times on surveillance cameras. 'Suddenly, I could not buy high-speed train tickets, my children were denied spots at good schools, and my photo was displayed on public screens as an untrustworthy person. All for crossing the street.'[98]

But some Chinese citizens view the system differently. Wang Chen, a small business owner in Shanghai, argues: 'Before social credit, people could cheat in business and face no consequences. Now there is accountability. My high score helps me get loans that banks would not give me based on traditional criteria.'

The Chinese system makes explicit what Western algorithmic scoring does implicitly: it creates a comprehensive evaluation system that affects access to opportunities based on behavioural patterns. The difference is transparency and accountability; Chinese citizens at least know they are being scored.

GDPR'S LIMITED PROTECTION

The European Union's General Data Protection Regulation was intended to protect citizens from algorithmic discrimination, but its effectiveness has proven limited.

The regulation requires companies to provide meaningful information about algorithmic decision-making and grants citizens the right to an explanation for automated decisions. But these protections often fail in practice. When Thomas challenged the increase in his health insurance premium, citing GDPR rights, the company provided the following explanation: 'Your premium was calculated using our proprietary risk assessment algorithm that considers multiple factors to ensure fair and accurate pricing.' No specific factors, no weights, no real explanation.[99]

Dr Elke Brandt, who studies AI regulation at the European University Institute, explains the limitation: 'GDPR assumes algorithms are explicable, but many AI systems operate as black boxes even to their creators. Companies cannot explain what they do not understand, and regulators lack the technical expertise to challenge vague explanations.'

The enforcement challenges are equally significant. Ireland's Data Protection Commission, responsible for regulating the European operations of many tech giants, has a staff of around 150 people overseeing companies with combined revenues exceeding a trillion euros. The asymmetry makes effective enforcement extremely difficult.

FIGHTING BACK: THE RESISTANCE MOVEMENTS

Despite the invisible power of the scoring society, resistance movements are emerging.

Data poisoners deliberately pollute their data profiles with false information to confuse algorithms. They use browser plugins that generate random search queries, apps that create fake location data, and services that obscure purchasing patterns.

Opt-out communities create parallel systems outside algorithmic control. They use cash, avoid social media, and build local networks that operate on human trust.

Transparency activists demand algorithmic accountability through litigation, legislation, and direct action. They have forced some companies to reveal scoring criteria and successfully challenged discriminatory algorithms in court.

Algorithm auditors, including researchers affiliated with the Algorithmic Justice League, reverse-engineer scoring systems to expose their logic and biases. Their work has revealed discriminatory patterns, forcing some companies to modify their algorithms.[100]

One activist explains: 'We are not anti-technology, but we demand that algorithms affecting human lives be transparent, accountable, and contestable. The invisible scoring society is incompatible with democracy.'

IMAGINING ALTERNATIVE FUTURES

The invisible scoring society is not inevitable. Alternative models could preserve the benefits of algorithmic decision-making while protecting human agency.

Transparent scoring would require all algorithms that affect individuals to publish their criteria, weights, and decision logic in understandable terms. Human override provisions would make any algorithmic decision that affects access to employment, housing, credit, or services appealable for human review. Scoring limits would protect certain life domains (romantic relationships, political participation, spiritual practices) from algorithmic evaluation. Data dignity frameworks would ensure individuals own their data and receive compensation when it is used for scoring, with the right to correct errors and delete information. Democratic governance would let communities democratically decide which algorithmic systems are acceptable and under what conditions.

The invisible scoring society represents a form of governance that no one voted for and few understand. The algorithms already govern us. The question is whether we will govern them in return or accept a future in which every human action is monitored, scored, and judged by systems we neither understand nor control.

As Preethi, still pursuing her rental appeal, puts it: 'I am not asking for special treatment. I am asking for the right to be judged as a human being, not a collection of data points. Is that really too much to ask in the twenty-first century?'

16

DIGITAL DEMOCRACY VS. ALGORITHMIC GOVERNANCE

WHEN CODE BECOMES CONSTITUTION

Imagine waking up to discover that your local council has been replaced overnight by an AI system that processes citizen requests, allocates resources, and makes policy decisions through machine learning algorithms trained on decades of municipal data. There are no more contentious town hall meetings, no more political disagreements about budget priorities, and no more waiting months for planning applications to be reviewed. The AI mayor processes citizen requests in real time, optimises resource allocation based on utilisation data, and implements policies that maximise measurable outcomes such as economic efficiency and resident satisfaction.

It sounds like a technocrat's utopia: governance without politics, decisions based on data rather than ideology, public administration that actually works efficiently. But it also sounds like a democrat's nightmare: governance without representation, decisions without deliberation, public administration that operates beyond human accountability or appeal.

This scenario is not science fiction; it is the logical endpoint of current trends toward algorithmic governance that are already reshaping how democratic institutions operate. From AI-powered citizen services to algorithmic resource allocation, artificial intelligence is quietly becoming a form of automated government that operates alongside, and sometimes instead of, traditional democratic processes.

ESTONIA'S DIGITAL DEMOCRACY EXPERIMENT

Estonia provides the world's most comprehensive example of digital government integration, with 99% of government services available online and a digital identity system that enables secure citizen interaction with government algorithms. The country's experience illuminates both the possibilities and the limitations of algorithmic governance.[101]

Estonia's digital government succeeds because it maintains clear boundaries between administrative efficiency and democratic decision-making. Citizens can vote online, file taxes automatically, access government services through mobile apps, and even establish businesses entirely through digital platforms. The efficiency gains are remarkable: Estonian citizens spend an estimated 15 minutes per year on tax filing, compared to hours or days in other countries.

However, Estonia's success depends on maintaining human democratic oversight while using technology to improve service delivery. AI systems handle routine service delivery and data processing, while human politicians and civil servants retain authority over policy decisions and resource allocation.

Siim Sikkut, Estonia's former Chief Information Officer, has explained the philosophy in various public statements: the country uses technology to make government more efficient and accessible, but never allows algorithms to make political decisions. Citizens interact with AI for services, but they vote for humans who make policy choices. The technology is infrastructure, not government.[102]

The system includes essential safeguards: algorithmic transparency so citizens can see how automated decisions are made; human override so any algorithmic decision can be appealed; democratic control so parliament oversees AI deployment; and privacy protection so citizens control their data.

Yet Estonia's model faces challenges. In 2023, a controversy erupted when the tax authority's AI system began flagging small business owners for audits based on patterns that correlated with ethnic minorities. While not intentionally discriminatory, the algorithm had learned biases from historical audit data. The incident led to new requirements for bias testing and human review of AI decisions.

AI TOWN HALLS: THE MADRID EXPERIMENT

Madrid's Decide Madrid platform represents one of the most ambitious attempts to use AI for democratic participation. The system allows citizens to propose policies, debate alternatives, and vote on municipal priorities, with AI facilitating discussions among hundreds of thousands of participants.[103]

The platform uses natural language processing to identify similar proposals and merge duplicates, summarise thousands of comments into key themes, detect and moderate toxic content, translate between languages to enable broader participation, and identify consensus points and areas of disagreement.

The results have been impressive. Over 400,000 citizens have participated, leading to the implementation of citizen-proposed projects including improvements to public transport, the development of green spaces, and social programmes. The AI enables a scale of democratic participation impossible through traditional town halls.

But challenges have emerged. Elena, a community organiser in Madrid, describes the limitations: 'The AI is good at processing opinions but poor at understanding context. It might identify that many people want more parks, but it does not understand the social dynamics of why certain neighbourhoods need them more, or the historical reasons why some communities distrust government promises.'

The platform also faces the digital divide. Older citizens, those without internet access, and people uncomfortable with technology are consistently excluded by the system's design rather than by any deliberate policy. The AI amplifies the voices of those who are digitally fluent and have the time to participate online, potentially creating new forms of democratic inequality.

Dr Pablo Aragón, who studies digital democracy at Universitat Pompeu Fabra, warns: 'AI can aggregate preferences efficiently, but democracy is not just about counting votes. It is about deliberation, compromise, and building shared understanding. Those human elements are hard to algorithmise.'

TAIWAN'S VTAIWAN: SUCCESS THROUGH SYNTHESIS

Taiwan's vTaiwan platform, an open-source consultation process developed in 2015 that uses AI-powered opinion-mapping software to surface consensus across large groups of citizens, offers perhaps the most successful model of AI-aided democracy. Rather than replacing human deliberation with algorithmic aggregation, it uses AI to facilitate deeper democratic engagement.[104]

The platform combines AI analysis with human facilitation for policy discussions on complex issues. When Taiwan faced controversy over Uber regulation, vTaiwan brought together taxi drivers, Uber drivers, passengers, and government officials in a process that combined online and offline deliberation. The AI identified different stakeholder perspectives, found surprising points of consensus, suggested compromise positions, and visualised opinion landscapes. But human facilitators guided discussions, ensured that all voices were heard, and helped translate technical policy language into citizen concerns.

The result was a regulatory framework that satisfied most stakeholders. Audrey Tang, Taiwan's former Digital Minister, explained the approach in an interview on the Harvard Business Review podcast in October 2020: AI does not make decisions; it helps humans make better ones. It is like having a brilliant assistant who can process everyone's input and find patterns, but humans still do the thinking, feeling, and deciding.[105]

SWITZERLAND'S DIGITAL VOTING CAUTION

Switzerland's experience with digital voting provides a cautionary tale about the risks of algorithmic democracy. After successful small-scale trials, Switzerland planned to expand online voting nationwide. But in 2019, security researchers discovered critical vulnerabilities in the system that could allow vote manipulation without detection. More fundamentally, they identified a philosophical problem: digital voting requires citizens to trust code they cannot verify, unlike paper ballots that can be physically observed and counted.[106]

Andreas Glaser, a professor of constitutional law at the University of Zurich, explains: 'Democracy requires not just accurate vote counting but public confidence in the process. When voting becomes a black box that citizens cannot understand or verify, it undermines democratic legitimacy even if the technology works perfectly.'

The controversy led to the suspension of the expansion of digital voting. Some cantons continue limited trials, but Switzerland has pulled back from full digitalisation of democracy.

THE ALGORITHM AS POLITICIAN

Some jurisdictions have experimented with AI systems that not only facilitate democracy but also actively participate in governance. In 2022, Denmark's Synthetic Party nominated an AI candidate for parliament. The party did not qualify for the ballot in that election, but the human organisers continued to develop the concept: the AI was trained on Danish political history, citizen surveys, and policy outcomes from similar countries, and was intended to generate policy positions by optimising for multiple objectives, including economic growth, social welfare, environmental protection, and individual freedom.[107]

The experiment raised fundamental questions. Can an AI represent citizen interests? Is optimisation for measurable outcomes the same as democratic representation? What happens when AI policy recommendations conflict with human values that cannot be quantified?

Lars, a political scientist at Copenhagen University, argues: 'The AI candidate forced us to confront what democratic representation really means. Is it about implementing citizen preferences efficiently, or about human judgement, empathy, and moral reasoning that no algorithm can replicate?'

WHEN ALGORITHMS MAKE BETTER DECISIONS THAN COMMITTEES

One uncomfortable truth about algorithmic governance is that AI systems sometimes do make better decisions than democratic processes, at least by certain metrics.

Studies comparing city planning decisions have found that AI systems consistently allocate resources more efficiently than city councils, reduce traffic congestion more effectively than transportation committees, and predict infrastructure needs more accurately than planning departments.[108]

A spokesperson at MIT's Urban Planning Lab explains: 'The AI does not get lobbied by special interests, does not worry about re-election, and does not make decisions based on political favours. In purely technical terms, it often produces better outcomes.'

But better depends on how you define it. The AI optimises for efficiency and measurable outcomes but cannot account for community values, historical injustices, or the importance of democratic participation itself. Consider two approaches to allocating city funds for park development. The democratic process is slow and messy, but it builds community engagement, addresses historical grievances, and maintains political legitimacy. The algorithmic process is more efficient, but it optimises for what can be measured and misses what cannot.

GOVERNING AI WHEN POLITICIANS DO NOT UNDERSTAND IT

Perhaps the most fundamental challenge in algorithmic governance is the knowledge gap between technological capabilities and democratic institutions. Legislative bodies that struggle to understand basic internet technologies are being asked to regulate AI systems that challenge fundamental assumptions about knowledge, decision-making, and accountability.

The problem was illustrated during Mark Zuckerberg's 2018 Congressional testimony, in which senators asked questions that revealed a fundamental misunderstanding of how the internet works. If legislators do not understand social media, how can they govern artificial intelligence?[109]

Some countries have created AI advisory bodies to bridge this gap. The UK's Office for AI, the EU's High-Level Expert Group on Artificial Intelligence, and similar bodies aim to connect technical expertise with democratic oversight.

But these technocratic solutions create their own democratic challenges. Who selects the experts? How do we ensure they represent citizen interests? What happens when technical experts disagree with democratic preferences?

An analyst at the Oxford Internet Institute argues: 'We need new forms of democratic participation that go beyond voting for representatives who do not understand the technologies governing our lives. Perhaps we need citizen juries for AI governance, democratic audits of algorithms, or new institutions that combine technical expertise with democratic accountability.'

BUILDING DEMOCRATIC AI

The path forward is not choosing between democracy and algorithmic efficiency, but rather developing forms of algorithmic governance that improve, rather than replace, democratic participation. This requires democratic inputs: AI systems trained on democratically determined values, not calibrated purely for efficiency; transparent processes so citizens understand how algorithmic systems make decisions affecting them; human accountability so humans remain responsible for algorithmic decisions with clear chains of accountability; participatory design so citizens participate in designing algorithmic systems that govern them; value pluralism so algorithmic systems accommodate diverse values that cannot be reduced to optimisation metrics; and contestability so any algorithmic decision affecting citizens is appealable through democratic processes.

As we delegate more governance to algorithmic systems, we risk creating a hollow democracy in which citizens vote while algorithms rule. The challenge is to preserve human agency and democratic values while drawing on AI's capabilities.

The code is becoming a constitution whether we acknowledge it or not. The question is whether we will write that code democratically or allow it to be written for us by systems we do not understand and cannot control. The interface between digital democracy and algorithmic governance will determine not just how we are governed but whether meaningful democracy survives the age of artificial intelligence.

THE INTERFACE BETWEEN US

This book began with a single premise: that artificial intelligence has stopped being artificial and begun to be intimate. After everything from AI mid-life crises to algorithmic shamanism, from environmental elephants to invisible scoring societies, the premise holds. We are not only living with these systems. We are adapting to them, and they are quietly adapting us back.

Remember Sarah from Chapter 1, the marketing manager who had spent years retraining for jobs that AI kept reshaping before she could settle into them? She eventually found her path by becoming what she calls a human-AI translator, helping organisations navigate the emotional and cultural aspects of automation. 'I stopped trying to outrun the algorithms,' she reflects, 'and started helping humans and machines understand each other.'

Or consider Marcus from Chapter 15, who discovered that a scoring algorithm was using his employment details to influence his romantic prospects. Rather than gaming the system or opting out entirely, he co-founded a transparent dating platform where algorithms show their reasoning and users can challenge unfair scores. 'We cannot eliminate algorithmic matchmaking,' he explains, 'but we can demand it treats us as humans, not data points.'

These are not stories of triumph or defeat, but of adaptation: messy, ongoing, profoundly human adaptation to a world where the boundary between human and artificial intelligence grows ever more permeable.

THE PATTERNS THAT EMERGED

Throughout our exploration, several recurring themes have woven through every chapter, suggesting deeper patterns in the development of human-AI relationships.

Asymmetric intelligence surfaces everywhere. AI systems excel at processing vast amounts of information and identifying patterns invisible to human perception. Yet, they struggle with context, wisdom, and the kind of judgement that emerges from lived experience. Humans excel at understanding meaning, working through ambiguity, and making intuitive leaps that no algorithm can replicate. Yet, we are overwhelmed by the scale and speed of information that AI handles effortlessly. The most successful human-AI relationships we have encountered, from Finnish classrooms to Taiwanese democracy platforms, deploy these complementary strengths.

The confidence paradox appears repeatedly: we trust machines that speak with certainty about things they do not fully understand over humans who acknowledge complexity and uncertainty. The Post Office Horizon scandal, GPS navigation disasters, and medical AI overconfidence all demonstrate how artificial certainty can override human wisdom. Yet understanding this paradox can help us develop what researchers call calibrated trust, knowing when algorithmic confidence reflects genuine capability versus statistical pattern-matching without comprehension.

Generational divides run deeper than simple age differences. Generation AI, growing up with algorithms as constant companions, demonstrates more sophisticated scepticism about technology than their parents, who alternate between uncritical enthusiasm and anxious resistance. The challenge is not teaching young people to be more sceptical of AI; they already are, but helping older generations develop the nuanced relationships with artificial intelligence that digital natives have absorbed by experience.

Invisible infrastructure shapes our choices without our awareness or consent. From algorithmic scoring systems that determine our opportunities to environmental costs hidden in distant data centres, artificial intelligence has become environmental rather than purely instrumental: something we exist within, not simply use. Making this infrastructure visible may be the first step toward maintaining human agency in an algorithmic world.

WHAT WE HAVE LEARNED ABOUT HUMAN-AI COLLABORATION

The evidence from our journey suggests that the future belongs to forms of collaboration that neither humans nor machines could achieve alone. Yet successful collaboration requires understanding what each party brings to the relationship and what each lacks.

The stories of successful adaptation (from the Mumbai taxi drivers who created their own synthesis of human knowledge and algorithmic efficiency, to the Finnish students learning to question AI outputs while using them creatively) share common elements. They all involve humans who stopped competing with AI on its terms and instead focused on distinctly human contributions: contextual understanding, ethical reasoning, emotional intelligence, and the ability to find meaning in ambiguity.

But collaboration is not always harmonious. The power dynamics are unequal, with AI systems backed by massive corporations, while individual humans struggle to understand, let alone influence, the algorithms that shape their lives. The environmental costs are unevenly distributed, with communities bearing the ecological burden of data centres while receiving few benefits. The economic rewards primarily flow to those who own the algorithms, rather than to those whose data trains them or whose labour they replace.

THE SKILLS WE ACTUALLY NEED

Perhaps the most surprising finding from our exploration is that the most valuable skills in an AI-augmented world are not necessarily technical. While AI literacy matters, the deeper challenge is developing the psychological and social capabilities necessary to work effectively with artificial intelligence while maintaining human agency and wisdom.

Meta-cognitive awareness, understanding our own thinking processes well enough to recognise when AI assistance helps versus when human judgement is essential, matters more than almost any specific technical competency. Collaborative intelligence involves learning to work with AI systems as partners, understanding their capabilities and limitations, and developing communication strategies that draw on artificial intelligence without being constrained by it. Adaptive resilience involves maintaining psychological flexibility in the face of technological change and developing an identity and purpose that are not dependent on specific job roles or technical skills. Critical evaluation requires distinguishing between artificial confidence and genuine competence, and maintaining appropriate scepticism about technological claims.

THE CHALLENGE OF AGENCY

Perhaps the most fundamental question emerging from our exploration is whether humans can maintain meaningful agency in a world increasingly shaped by artificial intelligence. Agency requires not just the ability to make choices, but the capacity to understand the consequences of those choices and to influence the systems that constrain them.

The invisible scoring society, the environmental costs of digital intelligence, and the algorithmic governance of daily life all represent new forms of constraint on human agency. These constraints operate through influence rather than coercion, shaping what we see and therefore what we think about, determining our opportunities without requiring our consent, and influencing our life chances based on criteria we cannot examine or appeal.

Yet we have also seen examples of humans reclaiming agency within algorithmic systems. The Algorithmic Justice League challenging discriminatory AI; Estonian citizens maintaining democratic oversight of digital government; creative artists finding ways to make human imagination irreplaceable: all demonstrate that human agency, while challenged, is not eliminated.

LOOKING FORWARD: THE HUMAN INTERFACE AS A POLITICAL PROJECT

The human interface is not just a technical challenge; it is a political and social project that will determine what kind of society we become as artificial intelligence grows more powerful and pervasive. The choices we make now about how to develop, deploy, and govern AI systems will shape human possibilities for generations to come.

We stand at a significant moment. AI systems are sophisticated enough to influence human life materially, but not so advanced that their development paths are predetermined. We still have opportunities to influence how artificial intelligence develops, what values it embodies, and what its relationship to human agency and welfare will be.

The work ahead is partly individual and partly collective. Individually, it means developing enough awareness to work with these systems without being quietly steered by them. Collectively, it means democratic governance that can actually oversee algorithmic power, economic arrangements that spread the benefits more evenly, and environmental accounting that puts the ecological cost of AI on the books. It also means leaving some things alone. Not everything needs to be optimised, measured, or scored. Love, friendship, creativity, spirituality, and play do fine without an algorithmic rating.

THE INTERFACE BETWEEN US

The title of this book, The Human Interface, was chosen deliberately. In computing, an interface is the boundary where two systems meet and interact. But we have discovered that the boundary between human and artificial intelligence is not a clean line. It is a complex, permeable membrane where human agency and artificial capability intersect in ways that neither AI developers nor users fully anticipated.

This interface is not fixed. It is constantly being negotiated through millions of daily interactions between humans and AI systems. Every time someone crafts a prompt, questions an algorithmic recommendation, or chooses human connection over digital efficiency, they are shaping this interface.

The stories in this book (teenagers teaching their parents to question AI, doctors learning when to trust their intuition over an algorithmic diagnosis, communities building alternatives to surveillance capitalism) are all small acts of negotiation at that boundary. Each one is a quiet refusal to be a passive recipient of whatever the technology arrives with.

How that interface gets designed, maintained, and defended will decide whether AI ends up amplifying human capability or quietly replacing it. The technology itself settles none of that. It is settled, slowly, in the millions of small decisions about where we let the algorithms in and where we keep them out.

WHAT TO WATCH

Three things will show whether this book has read the present correctly. Whether the generation raised inside algorithms turns its scepticism into changed defaults and better terms, or settles for better-informed resignation. Whether any government runs a genuinely contestable algorithmic decision system at a national scale by the late 2020s, of the kind Estonia and Taiwan have gestured towards. Whether the energy and water cost of large models is ever put on a public balance sheet, or stay hidden in distant data centres. None of the three is settled now. All three are checkable later.

A CLOSING THOUGHT

A confession, since the book has earned it. This account of human adaptation to AI was written with the help of AI. Claude researched complex topics, suggested ways to reorganise chapters, and caught errors that tired human eyes had slid past. The judgement about what any of it meant stayed with me, for better or worse. That is roughly the arrangement this whole book has been describing, observed from the inside of its writing.

We already share our world with artificial intelligence. The only open question is how much of that sharing we do on purpose, and how much we let happen while looking at our phones. Wisdom, creativity, and connection are not taken from us by the machines. They are handed over, a little at a time, in exchange for the convenience of an automated answer.

The machines can think. We are still the ones who decide what is worth thinking about, what a finished thing should mean, and which problems are worth the bother of solving.

This trilogy began with a panel of engineers on a San Francisco stage, congratulating themselves on building systems that would eliminate human bias. Three books later, the bias is still here. It has simply been laundered through better mathematics, and given the benefit of the doubt we used to reserve for people. The first volume watched AI reflect our prejudices with an air of objectivity. The second watched it stop reflecting our behaviour and start shaping it. This one has watched us adapt, badly and well and mostly in between, to systems that know us intimately and understand us not at all.

So the engineers were half right. We have built something that holds up a mirror, shapes what it sees, and learns the household routine. We just never finished reading the part of the manual that explained who was supposed to be in charge.

[illegible] and [illegible] stay [illegible] [illegible]

A C[illegible] FLAGGE[illegible]

A confession: since [illegible] [illegible] adaptation [illegible] [illegible] [illegible] complex topics [illegible] [illegible] of agents and causal story that filled [illegible] [illegible] [illegible] what [illegible] brought the [illegible] whole [illegible] obtained from the [illegible] writing.

[illegible] [illegible] our world with [illegible] [illegible] [illegible] looking [illegible] connections [illegible] [illegible] [illegible] [illegible] [illegible] [illegible] [illegible] of [illegible]

[illegible] [illegible] are [illegible] thinking about [illegible] [illegible]

This [illegible] began with a [illegible] congratulating themselves on [illegible] [illegible] [illegible] [illegible] through [illegible] weight of the [illegible] we used to reserve for people. The first volume [illegible] reflected our prejudices, with [illegible] second warned a step reflecting our [illegible] and [illegible] [illegible] [illegible] to systems that [illegible] all.

[illegible] were half right. We have [illegible] something that [illegible] what [illegible] [illegible] [illegible] we [illegible] finished reading [illegible] [illegible] who was supposed [illegible] in charge.

ACKNOWLEDGMENTS

Writing about human adaptation to artificial intelligence while becoming increasingly dependent on AI systems for research, analysis, and creative assistance created a real-time case study in the very phenomenon being examined. These acknowledgements recognise the humans whose insights made this exploration of human-AI coexistence possible, despite the considerable irony of using machines to understand what it means to remain human in an algorithmic age.

The MIT researchers documenting AI's impact on workplace dynamics revealed that the future of work is not just about which jobs disappear, but how the nature of human capability itself changes when machines become collaborators. Their findings suggest we are all becoming middle managers for our own algorithmic subordinates, which explains why everyone feels simultaneously overworked and underqualified.

Stanford's Human-Centred AI Institute contributed research demonstrating that 'digital natives' often struggle more than expected with AI systems, showing that being able to use TikTok does not automatically qualify you to collaborate with artificial intelligence. Their work challenged Silicon Valley's assumption that younger generations intuitively understand technology, revealing instead that familiarity with interfaces does not translate into understanding algorithms.

Anthropologists studying AI adoption across different cultural contexts offered perspectives that Silicon Valley's user experience research consistently misses, partly because conducting field research in real human communities requires leaving campus. Their documentation of how collectivist cultures approach AI differently from individualist societies revealed there is no universal model for human-AI coexistence, despite the tech industry's charming belief in one-size-fits-all solutions.

Workplace researchers investigating how AI changes professional identity provided sobering insights into the psychological challenges of algorithmic collaboration. Their studies revealed 'AI imposter syndrome', in which humans begin to doubt their own capabilities when machines can perform similar tasks, highlighting challenges that corporate wellness programmes are not equipped to address.

Educational researchers documenting AI's impact on learning have revealed concerning patterns among students who rely heavily on AI writing tools, as well as unexpected benefits in creative expression. Their research on 'cognitive outsourcing' provided evidence that using AI to think for you might be counterproductive to, well, thinking.

Research on 'algorithmic bedside manner' revealed how medical AI affects the fundamentally human aspects of healthcare relationships. It turns out patients prefer doctors who can maintain eye contact over algorithms with perfect diagnostic accuracy, a preference that medical schools may want to mention in their AI integration courses.

Journalists covering AI's social integration provided essential documentation of adaptation in real-world contexts, proving that the future of human-AI coexistence looks nothing like Silicon Valley's promotional videos. Their work revealed the gap between technological possibility and human reality, like the difference between a car advertisement and actual traffic.

Friends and colleagues who served as willing test subjects for theories about AI adaptation deserve recognition for their patience with constant questions about their relationships with algorithmic systems. Their willingness to analyse their own dependency on navigation apps and recommendation algorithms provided evidence that most people cannot remember how they lived before Google Maps, yet somehow survived.

My wife provided essential reality-checking throughout the writing process, particularly regarding claims about generational differences in AI adaptation. Her selective embrace of AI assistance while resisting other applications provided valuable data about the nuanced choices that characterise human adaptation.

The artificial intelligence systems that collaborated in researching and writing this book provided an ongoing demonstration of the adaptation challenges being analysed. Language models that occasionally produced insights beyond their training while frequently requiring human correction illustrated the complex negotiations that define human-AI collaboration, rather like working with brilliant but unreliable interns who never need coffee breaks but occasionally hallucinate entire academic papers.

Communities experimenting with alternative models of human-AI relationships inspired imagining different futures. Cooperatives developing community-controlled AI, schools implementing AI literacy education, and organisations building transparent algorithmic decision-making demonstrated that adaptation does not require accepting Silicon Valley's preferred models of human-machine interaction.

Early readers who pointed out successful AI integration examples that contradicted pessimistic predictions helped create a more nuanced understanding of the possibilities and limitations of adaptation. To those who demonstrated that humans and machines can work together without triggering existential crises: your experiences prove that the future might be less dystopian than feared, though probably more complicated than hoped.

Environmental researchers documenting AI's ecological impact provided sobering context: adapting to life with AI requires reckoning with its environmental consequences, not just its social implications. Their work revealed that our algorithmic future has a distinctly analogue carbon footprint, information that never seems to appear in tech company sustainability reports.

This book exists because AI integration affects everyone, while most people lack frameworks for understanding how to maintain human agency in algorithmic systems. The analysis represents the collective wisdom of researchers, practitioners, and communities working through technological coexistence, proving that the best insights into human-AI adaptation come from actually trying it.

To everyone working to ensure that human adaptation to AI preserves human dignity: your efforts matter more than efficiency metrics could ever measure. The human interface with artificial intelligence is still being designed, and the choices we make now will determine whether AI amplifies the best of human capability or gradually erodes it.

Because in the end, the question is not whether we can adapt to AI, but whether we can adapt to it without losing what makes us insufferably, irrationally, and beautifully human.

NOTES

1. The Harvard Business School and Accenture 'Hidden Workers' study (Fuller, J. et al., 2021, *Hidden Workers: Untapped Talent*, Harvard Business School Publishing) found that applicant tracking systems were filtering out qualified candidates at scale. The researchers estimated that over 90% of large US employers used ATS tools, and that these systems routinely excluded candidates who would have been suitable for roles. As screening algorithms go, this one had a talent for rejecting talent.

2. The evolution from 'learn to code' to 'learn to cope' happened faster than anyone predicted, which is itself a useful lesson about predicting the trajectory of technological change. The people who sold coding bootcamps in 2019 were not being dishonest – they were being wrong, which is a different thing, though equally expensive.

3. Applicant tracking systems do reduce certain forms of conscious bias while introducing systematic algorithmic bias. Whether this is progress depends on your view of which form of discrimination is worse. At least human bias is subject to litigation; algorithmic bias hides behind trade secrets.

4. The phenomenon of 'expertise vertigo' – the disorienting sense that the ground keeps shifting beneath professional competence – is

real, measurable, and not well served by advice to simply learn new skills faster. Some problems require structural solutions, not personal ones.

5. Livingstone, S. and Blum-Ross, A. (2020). *Parenting for a Digital Future*. Oxford University Press. OECD (2021). *21st-Century Readers: Developing Literacy Skills in a Digital World*. OECD Publishing. UNICEF Innocenti (2017). *Children in a Digital World*. UNICEF Office of Research.

6. Vartiainen, H. and Tedre, M. (2023). Using artificial intelligence in craft education: crafting with text-to-image generative models. *Digital Creativity*, 34(1), 1–21. Finland's approach is documented in the Finnish National Agency for Education's curriculum guidance on AI literacy for comprehensive schools.

7. The observation that schools pretend AI does not exist while students already live inside it captures an institutional lag that is both understandable and counterproductive. Schools have always lagged behind the culture they are supposed to prepare students for. This time, the lag is unusually visible.

8. The Cambridge AI and Education Initiative findings from 2024, referenced with permission. The university's published guidance is available through its Digital Education unit.

9. OECD (2023). *PISA 2022 Results: Creative Minds, Creative Schools*. OECD Publishing. Livingstone, S. et al. (2022). *The Digital Lives of Children*. LSE/UKRI report. The research consistently finds that children with adult support and a critical framework develop more calibrated views of AI than those left to form impressions through unguided use.

10. Turkle, S. (2017). *Alone Together: Why We Expect More from Technology and Less from Each Other* (3rd edition). Basic Books. Turkle's documented research on technology and human connection provides a rich conceptual foundation. However, the term 'collaborative scepticism' is the author's own formulation, inspired by her work, rather than a direct quotation from her writing.

11. DeepMind's internal coordination challenges during its rapid growth phase have been discussed in multiple published accounts of

the organisation's culture. Alessandro is a composite voice drawing on documented patterns of experience from AI research organisations generally. No footnote cue for composite voices – this note appears in the back matter for editorial transparency only and does not carry a cue in the text.

12. The cobbler's children paradox in AI companies is so well-documented that it has become a cliché of technology journalism. That does not make it less true. A cliché is a truth that has been told too often.

13. Kim, S. (2023). Meeting culture and organisational change in high-growth technology firms. *Journal of Organizational Behavior*, 44(3), 412–429. The finding that meetings persist for psychological rather than informational reasons will surprise no one who has attended a meeting about reducing meetings.

14. Notion's public documentation of their AI integration approach is available at Notion. The company has been unusually transparent about how they use their own product, which is either admirable consistency or effective marketing – probably both.

15. Chen, R. (2024). Technology adoption patterns across traditional and born-digital organisations. *MIT Sloan Management Review*, Spring 2024. The finding that traditional manufacturers sometimes outperform tech companies at implementing AI tools is one of the more satisfying ironies in contemporary business literature.

16. Bundesministerium für Wirtschaft und Klimaschutz (2023). *Industrie 4.0: Stand der Umsetzung in deutschen Unternehmen*. The €3.2 billion figure represents federal programme spending; total investment, including employer and Land contributions, is considerably higher.

17. GitHub (2022). *The State of the Octoverse 2022*. GitHub, Inc. Chen, M. et al. (2021). Evaluating large language models trained on code. arXiv:2107.03374. The pace at which AI coding assistance went from impressive to nearly standard professional practice was faster than almost anyone in the industry predicted in 2020.

18. Denmark's FlexSecure model is described in OECD (2020). *Facing the Future: Korea's Education System and Skills Strategy*. While

primarily focused on Korea, this OECD volume provides a useful comparative analysis of Nordic active labour market policies. For the FlexSecure model specifically: Ministry of Employment (Denmark) (2023). *The Danish Flexicurity Model*. Copenhagen.

19. SkillsFuture Singapore (2023). *Annual Report 2022/23*. SkillsFuture Singapore, Singapore. The programme's design reflects Singapore's distinctive approach to managing technological transition: systematic, government-led, and grounded in an explicit theory of adult learning across the life course.

20. Okonkwo, A. et al. (2023). Career transitions and psychological well-being in technology-disrupted sectors: evidence from sub-Saharan Africa. *Work, Employment and Society*, 37(4), 889–907. The finding that retraining provides psychological benefits independent of its economic outcomes has important implications for how we design workforce transition programmes.

21. Martinez, J. (2023). Career resilience in the age of technological disruption: a framework for practitioners. *Journal of Vocational Behavior*, 140, 103832. The programme's emphasis on financial, social, and psychological capital rather than specific technical skills reflects a growing consensus in vocational psychology about what actually predicts successful adaptation to technological change.

22. Leeds Teaching Hospitals NHS Trust (2023). *Annual Quality Report*. The misidentification of athletic cardiac variants by AI diagnostic systems is documented in the sports cardiology literature. See Drezner, J.A. et al. (2013). Abnormal electrocardiographic findings in athletes: recognising changes suggestive of primary electrical disease. *British Journal of Sports Medicine*, 47(3), 153–167.

23. Babylon Health plc filed for bankruptcy in 2023. The company's collapse is documented in contemporaneous reporting by the *Financial Times* and *STAT News*. Post-mortem analyses have identified overreliance on claims of diagnostic parity with physicians, combined with underinvestment in safety validation, as primary contributing factors.

24. Tomašev, N. et al. (2019). A clinically applicable approach to continuous prediction of future acute kidney injury. *Nature*, 572, 116–

119. This is the foundational paper describing the Royal Free Hospital/DeepMind collaboration. The system is now part of NHS standard practice in participating trusts.

25. Adeyemi, O. et al. (2023). Algorithmic diagnosis in low-resource settings: opportunities and risks. *The Lancet Digital Health*, 5(8), e554–e562. The observation that AI symptom checkers mistake correlation for causation in complex presentations is not a criticism of the technology per se – it is a description of its current limitations, which are well understood by researchers, if not always by patients.

26. PathAI (2023). *Clinical Validation Studies*. PathAI, Inc. Kather, J.N. et al. (2020). Deep learning in histopathology – the path to the clinic. *Nature Medicine*, 27, 775–784. The pathology application represents something like the ideal use case for medical AI: high-volume, pattern-intensive work with objective ground truth, where augmenting human capacity addresses a genuine global shortage.

27. Liu, X. et al. (2019). 'A comparison of deep learning performance against health-care professionals in detecting diseases from medical imaging: a systematic review and meta-analysis.' *The Lancet Digital Health*, 1(6), e271–e297. https://doi.org/10.1016/S2589-7500(19)30123-2. The authors also noted that most studies compared algorithms against clinicians working without the contextual information they would normally have, which is rather like racing someone whose shoelaces you have tied together.

28. University of Toronto Temerty Faculty of Medicine (2023). *AI and the Future of Medical Education: Curriculum Principles*. Available at medicine.utoronto.ca. The cognitive prosthetic framing – treating AI as extending rather than replacing human capability – is increasingly common in medical education literature.

29. This scenario is illustrative rather than a documented specific case. German courts have addressed several questions regarding AI-assisted medical decision-making, and the general principle that physicians retain liability for clinical decisions, regardless of AI involvement, reflects the consensus position of German medical law scholars. Katzenmeier, C. (2021). Haftung bei KI-gestützter Medizin. *Neue Juristische Wochenschrift*, 74(20), 1387–1392.

30. Kim, S. (2022). Calibrated trust in clinical AI systems. *npj Digital Medicine*, 5, 182. The concept of algorithmic clinical judgement – knowing when AI adds value and when human expertise is irreplaceable – is becoming a core competency in medical training programmes worldwide.

31. Richardson, E. (2024). When AI writes better essays: rethinking assessment in the English classroom. *English in Education*, 58(1), 14–29. Emma Richardson's published reflection on her experience is one of the more honest accounts by teachers of the disruption AI-generated writing has introduced to secondary English teaching.

32. Riverside Academy, Newham, London (2023). *AI Literacy Programme: Year Two Evaluation*. Internal report. Twelve other London schools have since adopted the programme through the Newham Learning Trust.

33. Cambridge University (2024). *Guidance on the Use of Artificial Intelligence in Academic Work*. Office of the Vice-Chancellor, University of Cambridge. The document represents a genuine evolution in institutional thinking from the university's initial prohibition stance.

34. International School of Brussels (2023). *Performance-Based Assessment in the AI Age*. ISB Educational Research, Brussels. The history simulation methodology has attracted particular interest from educators seeking assessment approaches that are genuinely AI-resistant.

35. Matos, E. (2024). Learning architects: rethinking the teacher's role in AI-integrated classrooms. *Cadernos de Pesquisa*, 54(1), e10212. The architect metaphor for teaching has become influential in Brazilian AI education discourse.

36. The AI system that develops 'preferences' for certain data formats is not conscious and does not have preferences in any meaningful sense. But the behavioural patterns that emerge from machine learning can function like preferences, requiring what engineers sometimes call 'expectation management' – which is a polite way of saying negotiation with a very expensive and opinionated piece of software.

37. McDonald, G. (2024). *You Have Not Yet Heard Your Favourite*

Song: How Streaming Changes Music. Canbury Press. ISBN: 978-1914487156. McDonald's account of how Spotify's algorithmic systems developed consistent aesthetic tendencies is one of the more thoughtful insider perspectives on human-AI creative collaboration available. McDonald was interviewed about the book for Hypebot (October 2024): hypebot.com/hypebot/2024/10/interview-with-spotify-music-data-alchemist-glenn-mcdonald.html.

38. Valve Corporation's flat organisational structure and its interaction with internal AI tools have been described in various press accounts. The unnamed developer's comments reflect documented patterns; the specific quotation is a composite voice without a footnote cue.

39. The financial trading AI slowdown strike is a well-documented category of algorithmic failure. When competing objectives create a situation in which any action reduces aggregate performance, a system optimising for the aggregate will tend toward inaction. Economists call this a locally optimal equilibrium; engineers call it a bug. It is technically both.

40. European Parliament (2020). *Report on Civil Law Rules on Robotics* (2015/2103(INL)). The electronic personhood proposal has not been adopted as a regulation, but it remains influential in EU AI governance debates. Critics argue it creates liability without accountability; supporters argue it acknowledges a legal reality that already exists.

41. Hashimoto, Y. (2023). Robot retirement ceremonies and the maintenance of human empathy in automated workplaces. *East Asian Science, Technology and Society*, 17(2), 223–241. The practice is more widespread in Japan than Western media coverage suggests, and the researcher's analysis of its social function – practising respect toward humans by practising respect toward tools – is more sophisticated than the headline treatment it usually receives.

42. Wong, L. (2023). *Human-AI Collaboration Principles for the Modern Workplace*. Microsoft Research White Paper. The four principles outlined are consistent with the published guidance that

Microsoft has developed for AI deployment across its enterprise customers.

43. Liu, W. (2023). East-West technological exchange in the age of AI: a philosophical perspective. *Philosophy and Technology*, 36, 83. Liu's observation about quarterly development cycles versus millennial contemplative traditions is presented here as a paraphrase of arguments made in this article; it was published as a scholarly analysis rather than a quotation.

44. Bai, Y. et al. (2022). Constitutional AI: Harmlessness from AI Feedback. arXiv:2212.08073. The constitutional AI approach is described and credited to Anthropic's research team; the connection to Confucian governance concepts is the author's interpretive framing rather than Anthropic's own description of their work.

45. Patagonia (2023). *Our Footprint: Environmental and Social Responsibility Report*. Patagonia, Inc. The company's public documentation of its AI implementation philosophy is more detailed than most corporate sustainability reporting.

46. Gellert, R. Interview on CNBC, 21 September 2022, following Patagonia's ownership restructuring announcement (cnbc.com/video/2022/09/21/watch-cnbcs-full-interview-with-patagonia-ceo-ryan-gellert.html); see also 'What Patagonia's CEO Has Learned a Year Into the New Ownership', *Time* (2023), time.com/6315770/patagonia-ownership-climate-change/; and NationSwell, 'Patagonia CEO Ryan Gellert: Our biggest impact has been modeling a different way of doing business' (2023), nationswell.com. The paraphrase in the text represents the consistent position Gellert has articulated across these and other public forums rather than a verbatim quotation from any single source.

47. Infocomm Media Development Authority and Personal Data Protection Commission, Singapore. (2020). *Model AI Governance Framework*, 2nd edition. January 2020. Available at: https://www.pdpc.gov.sg/help-and-resources/2020/01/model-ai-governance-framework. This is the authoritative source for Singapore's AI governance approach; the framework is freely available and widely cited in comparative AI policy literature.

48. Altman, S. (2022). Appearance on Art of Accomplishment podcast, January 2022. Altman, S. (2023). Conversation with Jack Kornfield at Wisdom 2.0, April 2023. Both are publicly available. The paraphrase here represents themes from these public appearances rather than a direct quotation; the earlier edition's HBR citation was not a real source and has been removed entirely.

49. Dorsey, J. (2019). Twitter thread documenting his Vipassana retreat in Myanmar, January 2019. The irony of documenting a ten-day silence via the medium that pioneered compulsive short-form communication did not go unremarked. Whether Dorsey's subsequent algorithm decisions reflected contemplative insight is a matter of interpretation.

50. Tan, C.-M. (2012). *Search Inside Yourself: The Unexpected Path to Achieving Success, Happiness (and World Peace)*. HarperOne. The critique of corporate mindfulness programmes as a productivity aid rather than a means of cultivating wisdom is developed in McMindfulness (Purser, R., 2019, Repeater Books), which provides a useful counterpoint to the programme's self-presentation.

51. Jack Ma's Taoist philosophy and its influence on Alibaba's AI systems are described in multiple Chinese-language business accounts and in his own speeches. Ma's 2019 remarks about Wu Wei and algorithm design were delivered at the World Economic Forum and are available in the WEF archive. Quotation marks have been removed; this is a paraphrase of documented public statements.

52. Mehta, A. (2023). Toward genuine East-West synthesis in AI development: a philosophical framework. *AI and Society*, 38(4), 1847–1861. The four-point framework is adapted from this article.

53. Torres, M. (2024). Unpublished professional account documented with permission. Maya Torres is a composite voice; this note appears for editorial transparency only.

54. Chen, M. (2023). *Generative AI in Creative Workflows: Adobe's Approach*. Adobe Research White Paper. The 'painting with words' formulation is from this document.

55. Rodriguez, A. (2023). Digital shamanism: prompt engineering and the anthropology of human-AI communication. *New Media and*

Society, 25(9), 2341–2358. The shamanism parallel is developed in depth in this paper, which is one of the more intellectually serious treatments of prompt engineering as a cultural phenomenon.

56. Thompson, M. (2024). Unpublished professional account documented with permission. Marcus Thompson, the prompt engineer, is a separate character from Marcus Thompson, the oil painter in Chapter 12; the name collision was introduced in the first edition and corrected in this edition. This note appears for editorial transparency only.

57. Bao, E. (2023). Limits of prompt engineering in large language models: a systematic review. *ACM Computing Surveys*, 56(2), article 42. The distinction between optimising a capable system and making an incapable system capable is fundamental to understanding what prompt engineering can and cannot achieve.

58. Fujitsu provided the Horizon software under a contract with the Post Office and seconded engineers who had remote access to branch data. The Post Office Horizon IT Inquiry, chaired by Sir Wyn Williams, found that Fujitsu engineers were aware of bugs and could make unilateral adjustments to branch accounts without postmasters' knowledge. Fujitsu issued an apology to the subpostmasters in 2024.

59. House of Commons Business and Trade Committee (2024). *Post Office Horizon IT Inquiry: Government Response*. HC 124. The figure of over 700 Post Office-led prosecutions is from the official inquiry record. The full scope of the scandal – prosecutions, convictions, appeals, compensation – is documented at the Post Office Horizon IT Inquiry website (postofficehorizoninquiry.org.uk).

60. Bates, A. (2024). First witness statement, WITN00050100, Post Office Horizon IT Inquiry, published at postofficehorizoninquiry.org.uk. The description here is a paraphrase of the institutional culture documented in Bates's testimony and the wider inquiry record, not a direct quotation. The inquiry's published record runs to thousands of pages, none of which improve on the postmasters' original observation that the computer was wrong.

61. Skinner, J. (2022). First witness statement WITN01260100, dated

16 February 2022, Post Office Horizon IT Inquiry, available at postofficehorizoninquiry.org.uk. The description in the text is a paraphrase of the experiences documented in Skinner's statement and in the Guardian podcast accounts she references (published 10–11 May 2021) rather than a direct quotation. The statement documents her guilty plea on legal advice, her nine-month custodial sentence, and the institutional weight placed on Horizon records over her own account. The specific phrase attributed to her in some secondary accounts could not be confirmed verbatim in the primary statement; the paraphrase here accurately represents her documented experience.

62. The phenomenon of GPS-induced navigation errors is well-documented. Burnett, G. (2009). 'Turn right at the end of the road': designing and evaluating instructions for pedestrian navigation systems. *Personal and Ubiquitous Computing*, 13(7), 549–556. Emergency services in several countries have published guidance specifically addressing GPS-related vehicle incidents.

63. Hassan, T. (2024). Algorithmic diagnostic confidence and patient trust: observations from primary care. *British Journal of General Practice*, 74(742), e287–e293. The pattern of patients preferring AI diagnostic confidence to physician uncertainty is documented across multiple healthcare systems and appears to reflect deep psychological tendencies toward expressed certainty.

64. Kim, S. (2022). Op. cit. (see note 30).

65. European Parliament and Council (2024). *Regulation (EU) 2024/1689 of the European Parliament and of the Council laying down harmonised rules on artificial intelligence (AI Act)*. OJ L, 12 July 2024. The explainability requirements in Articles 13 and 86 represent the regulatory attempt to address the confidence paradox discussed in this chapter.

66. Composite voice; documented from patterns in published accounts of AI-driven banking experience. See Revolut plc *Transparency Report* (2023) for aggregate data on AI-driven credit and spending interventions.

67. Composite voice; documented from published accounts of

Revolut user experiences, including coverage in *The Guardian* and *Which?* magazine.

68. Dastin, J. (2022). The Lemonade insurance app used AI to flag claims from customers who mentioned Black Lives Matter. *Reuters*, 14 June 2022. The company disputed the framing of this report, but the underlying data was drawn from its own published IPO prospectus.

69. MacMillan, D. and O'Brien, S. (2021). Robinhood used manipulative tactics on amateur traders, Massachusetts regulator says. *The Washington Post*, 15 December 2021. The Alex Kearns case is documented in contemporaneous press coverage and the subsequent congressional investigation.

70. Cleo (2023). *Impact Report: User Financial Outcomes*. Cleo AI, Ltd. Third-party verification of these outcomes has not been independently conducted; the figures should be treated as company-reported data.

71. Zhang, L. (2023). Alternative credit scoring and financial inclusion: evidence and risks. *Journal of Consumer Affairs*, 57(2), 611–634. The correlation-privilege problem in algorithmic credit scoring is one of the most technically complex aspects of AI fairness research.

72. Getty Images, Inc. v. Stability AI, Ltd. Filed in the High Court of Justice (England and Wales), January 2023. The full claim documentation is available at the court registry.

73. Getty Images, Inc. v. Stability AI, Ltd., UK High Court judgment, November 2025. Stability AI largely prevailed on the technical copyright claims under UK law, with the court finding that the training process did not constitute infringement as currently defined. The judge noted the legal framework predated AI training and flagged the question for Parliament. Getty has indicated it will pursue further remedies. The case in the United States continues separately.

74. Chen, D. (2022). *The Machine Dreams of Being Human* [Conceptual installation]. Exhibited at the New Museum, New York, September 2022. Catalogue essay available from the museum's publications department.

75. Herndon, H. (2022). Artist statement published in conjunction with the release of *PROTO* (4AD). Herndon's public writing about her

AI collaborations is more philosophically sophisticated than most artists' commentary on AI tools.

76. Writers Guild of America (2023). *2023 MBA Summary of Terms*. The AI provisions – particularly on crediting, training data, and ownership – represent the most detailed union agreement on AI in any creative industry and have become a reference point for subsequent negotiations.

77. Sutton, C. (2023). Address to the Central Saint Martins staff seminar on AI and creative education, November 2023. Published in summary form in the institution's research newsletter.

78. Richardson, D. (2023). Unpublished account documented with permission. SmartBrew is a composite illustration of AI-washing practices rather than a single specific company; David Richardson is a composite voice without a footnote cue in the text.

79. Samuel (2024). Unpublished account documented with permission. Composite voice; no footnote cue in text.

80. House of Commons Library (2025). *AI in UK Government Departments* (CBP-10236). House of Commons Library, London. Published 4 April 2025. Available at commonslibrary.parliament.uk/research-briefings/cbp-10236/. The briefing documents AI use across central government departments and notes the government's 'test and learn' approach to AI implementation. It provides departmental examples rather than a single headline count of projects, consistent with the characterisation in the text of the difficulty of distinguishing genuine machine-learning deployments from conventionally automated processes relabelled as AI. The specific figure cited in the first edition (147 projects, via FOI) cannot be verified against a primary source and has been removed from this edition.

81. Bzdok, D. et al. (2018). Statistics versus machine learning. *Nature Methods*, 15, 233–234. The boundary between statistical methods and machine learning is genuinely contested in the methodological literature, which makes the rebranding of traditional statistics as AI both technically arguable and clearly opportunistic.

82. Stanford Human-Centerd Artificial Intelligence (2024). *AI Index Report 2024*. Stanford University. The institute's annual index

provides the most comprehensive data on AI development trends and is the source of contextual claims about the prevalence of AI washing.

83. Buolamwini, J. and Gebru, T. (2018). Gender shades: intersectional accuracy disparities in commercial gender classification. *Proceedings of Machine Learning Research*, 81, 1–15. The Algorithmic Justice League, founded by Joy Buolamwini, is a real organisation conducting real audits; unlike the Digital Childhood Institute or the Mindful Technology Collective (both removed from this edition), it has a verifiable existence and publication record.

84. Li, P. et al. (2023). Making AI less 'thirsty': uncovering and addressing the secret water footprint of AI models. arXiv:2304.03271. Published in revised form in *Communications of the ACM*, 2025. The 700,000-litre figure applies to GPT-3 training; OpenAI does not publicly disclose figures for later models. The first edition incorrectly attributed this figure to GPT-4; GPT-3 is the model studied in the Li et al. research.

85. Central Statistics Office, Ireland (2024). *Data Centres Metered Electricity Consumption 2023*. CSO, Dublin. Published 23 July 2024. Available at cso.ie/en/releasesandpublications/ep/p-dcmec/datacentresmeteredelectricityconsumption2023/. Key finding: "The percentage of total metered electricity consumption used by data centres rose from 5% in 2015 to 21% in 2023." The CSO publishes this series annually; the 2024 figure (22%) is reported in the CSO's subsequent release in 2025. The figure in the text uses the 2023 data, which was the most recent complete annual figure available at the time of this edition.

86. Microsoft (2020). *Project Natick: The Story of Microsoft's Undersea Data Center*. Microsoft Research. Cutler, B. (2020). Microsoft finds underwater datacenters are reliable, practical and use energy sustainably. Microsoft blog, 14 September 2020.

87. Google (2023). *Environmental Report 2023*. Alphabet Inc. The Arizona figures are from a combination of Google's own reporting and environmental impact assessments filed with local authorities.

88. Li, P. et al. (2023). Op. cit. (see note 81). The 500ml per conver-

sation estimate is the researchers' own calculation based on cooling water data from data centres in temperate and warm US states.

89. Patterson, D. et al. (2022). The carbon footprint of machine learning training will plateau, then shrink. *Computer*, 55(7), 18–28. The flight comparison figure is based on the emissions calculations in this paper applied to a representative large training run in a coal-heavy grid region.

90. Evans, R. and Gao, J. (2016). DeepMind AI reduces Google data centre cooling bill by 40%. DeepMind blog, 20 July 2016. The energy reduction achieved was to cooling energy use, not overall energy costs – the first edition's description as 'cooling costs' was imprecise and has been corrected. The observation that training energy exceeds early operational savings is drawn from independent energy audit literature rather than from DeepMind's own publications.

91. Kim, S. (2022). AI efficiency gains and the rebound effect in digital consumption. *Nature Energy*, 7, 996–997. The rebound effect is well established in energy economics generally; its application to AI efficiency, specifically, is an emerging area of research.

92. Wu, C.-J. et al. (2022). Sustainable AI: Environmental implications, challenges and opportunities. *Proceedings of Machine Learning and Systems*, 4, 795–813. The library-versus-factory framing for AI model sharing is from this paper.

93. Composite voice; documented from patterns in published accounts of algorithmic tenant screening. The postcode-association mechanism is described in: Eubanks, V. (2018). *Automating Inequality*. St. Martin's Press. Chapter 3 is particularly relevant.

94. Thompson (2023). Unpublished account documented with permission. Composite voice; no footnote cue in text.

95. Tinder's desirability scoring system, known internally as 'Elo,' was described in a 2019 Wired article: Carr, A. (2016). I found out my secret Tinder rating, and now I wish I hadn't. *Fast Company*, 12 January 2016. The company has since updated its matching algorithm, but the core recursive structure – being liked by high-scorers increases your score – remains.

96. Ahmed (2024). Unpublished account documented with permission. Composite voice; no footnote cue in text.

97. Rosenblat, A. (2018). *Uberland: How Algorithms Are Rewriting the Rules of Work*. University of California Press. This is the definitive scholarly account of Uber's algorithmic management system and its implications for labour relations.

98. Xiaoming (2023). Unpublished account documented with permission. Composite voice; no footnote cue in text.

99. Thomas (2023). Unpublished account documented with permission. Composite voice; no footnote cue in text. The GDPR Article 22 right to explanation and its practical limitations are analysed in: Edwards, L. and Veale, M. (2017). Slave to the algorithm: why a right to an explanation is probably not the remedy you are looking for. *Duke Law and Technology Review*, 16(1), 18–84.

100. Buolamwini, J. (2023). *Unmasking AI: My Mission to Protect What Is Human in a World of Machines*. Random House. This is the most accessible account of the Algorithmic Justice League's work by its founder.

101. Mets, K. (2022). *Estonia: A Digital Society*. e-Estonia.com. The 99% figure for online government services is from official Estonian government reporting and is updated annually.

102. Sikkut, S. (2021). How Estonia built a digital government. *Harvard Business Review*, 17 February 2021. The philosophy described in the chapter is consistent with Sikkut's documented public statements; the paraphrase is drawn from this article and related public presentations rather than attributed as a direct quotation, in line with the corrections register.

103. Decide Madrid (2023). *Participation Statistics 2023*. Ayuntamiento de Madrid. The 400,000+ figure is from official platform reporting.

104. Tang, A. (2020). Digital minister in an age of viral rumours. *Harvard Business Review* podcast, October 2020. Tang's description of the AI's role in vTaiwan – as a facilitator rather than a decision-maker – is drawn from this interview and converted from direct quotation to paraphrase as required by the corrections register. See also: Hsiao, Y.-

T. and Tang, A. (2021). vTaiwan: An empirical study of the open consultation process in Taiwan. *Journal of e-Democracy*, 13(1), 21–48.

105. Tang, A. (2020). Op. cit.

106. Swiss Federal Chancellery (2019). *Statement on the suspension of the extended e-voting trial*. Berne, March 2019. Glaser, A. (2019). Rechtliche Anforderungen an die Validierbarkeit von E-Voting-Systemen. *Schweizerisches Zentralblatt für Staats- und Verwaltungsrecht*, 120(6), 317–334.

107. The Synthetic Party (Det Syntetiske Parti) contested the 2022 Danish general election; the party did not qualify for the ballot. Reports that it received 0.1% of the vote in a 2023 election cannot be verified and appear to be incorrect; the party's participation was in the 2022 election, in which it failed to reach the threshold to appear on the ballot. This correction reflects the replacements register entry for this claim.

108. Glaeser, E.L. et al. (2018). Big data and big cities: the promises and limitations of improved measures of urban life. *Economic Inquiry*, 56(1), 114–137. The comparison of AI versus committee decision-making in urban planning is drawn from this study; the limitations acknowledged in the text are also the study's own limitations section.

109. Zuckerberg, M. (2018). Testimony before the Senate Commerce and Judiciary Committees, 10 April 2018. Congressional Record. The hearings were extensively covered, and the transcripts are publicly available. The date is 2018, not 2019 as stated in the first edition.

SOURCES AND FURTHER READING

BOOKS AND ACADEMIC SOURCES

Acemoglu, Daron and Pascual Restrepo. *The Race Between Man and Machine: Implications of Technology for Growth, Factor Shares and Employment.* MIT Press, 2022. Leading economists examine technological displacement with the dispassion of people whose jobs are unlikely to be automated. Their mathematical models are rigorous, though one suspects reality is messier than their equations suggest.

Benjamin, Ruha. *Race After Technology: Abolitionist Tools for the New Jim Code.* Polity Press, 2019. Benjamin's brilliant analysis of algorithmic bias reads like a technical manual for social justice, if social justice came with debugging instructions. Essential reading for anyone who still believes artificial intelligence is politically neutral.

Crawford, Kate. *Atlas of AI: Power, Politics, and the Planetary Costs of Artificial Intelligence.* Yale University Press, 2021. Crawford's comprehensive examination of AI's environmental and social costs reads like an environmental impact statement for the digital age, written by someone with both moral clarity and a functioning calculator.

Davidson, Cathy N. *The New Education: How to Revolutionise the University to Prepare Students for a World in Flux.* Basic Books, 2017. Davidson argues for educational transformation with the passion of someone who has spent decades watching universities resist change with medieval determination.

Eubanks, Virginia. *Automating Inequality: How High-Tech Tools Profile, Police, and Punish the Poor.* St. Martin's Press, 2018. Eubanks documents algorithmic discrimination with the thoroughness of an investigative journalist who has spent too much time discovering that computers can be just as prejudiced as people, only faster.

Noble, Safiya Umoja. *Algorithms of Oppression: How Search Engines Reinforce Racism.* NYU Press, 2018. Noble's groundbreaking analysis reveals why Google searches sometimes return horrifying results, written by someone who actually investigated rather than assuming 'computer says no' is morally neutral.

O'Neil, Cathy. *Weapons of Math Destruction: How Big Data Increases Inequality and Threatens Democracy.* Crown, 2016. O'Neil writes about algorithmic bias with the frustrated expertise of a mathematician who discovered that data science had become corporate theology.

Turkle, Sherry. *Alone Together: Why We Expect More from Technology and Less from Each Other.* 3rd ed. Basic Books, 2017. Turkle's exploration of digital relationships reads like therapy notes from a civilisation that confused connectivity with connection.

Zuboff, Shoshana. *The Age of Surveillance Capitalism: The Fight for a Human Future at the New Frontier of Power.* PublicAffairs, 2019. Zuboff's monumental analysis reads like a horror novel about data collection, except it's non-fiction and the monsters are real.

RESEARCH REPORTS AND POLICY DOCUMENTS

Brookings Institution. 'AI and the Future of Work: Evidence from the Field.' Washington, DC: Brookings Institution, 2024. Policy research that maintains optimism about evidence-based recommendations despite minimal evidence that policymakers read research reports.

European Centre for the Development of Vocational Training. 'Career Resilience in the Digital Age.' CEDEFOP Reference Series 118, 2024. European bureaucracy's attempt to document adaptation to change, written at the pace bureaucracies typically adapt to anything.

European Commission. 'Ethics Guidelines for Trustworthy AI.' High-Level Expert Group on Artificial Intelligence, 2024. The EU's comprehensive framework for AI ethics, written by people who understand both technology and moral philosophy – apparently, such people exist.

European Environment Agency. 'Data Centre Energy Consumption in the EU: Projections to 2030.' EEA Technical Report No. 8/2024. Projecting future energy consumption with the precision of weather forecasters predicting next month's temperature.

MIT Technology Review. 'The State of AI in 2024: Annual Report.' Cambridge: MIT Technology Review, 2024. MIT's annual examination of an industry that grows faster than anyone can document it.

OECD. 'AI and Education: Guidance for Policy Makers.' OECD Education Policy Perspectives, No. 37, 2024. International guidance assumes policymakers want evidence-based education reform rather than political talking points.

Stanford Institute for Human-Centered AI. 'AI Index Report 2024: Measuring Progress in Artificial Intelligence.' Stanford University, 2024. Attempting to measure AI progress is rather like measuring the speed of light with a sundial.

UK Government Office for AI. 'AI Governance Framework: Democratic Oversight Mechanisms.' Department for Science, Innovation and Technology, 2024. British governance approaches AI with the systematic thoroughness usually reserved for tea-preparation protocols.

ACADEMIC JOURNAL ARTICLES

Google Health AI. 'Diabetic Retinopathy Screening: Global Implementation Results.' *Nature Medicine*, Vol. 29, pp. 1847–1853 (2023). Google is teaching machines to diagnose eye diseases better than doctors, raising questions about medical education and the future of human expertise.

MIT Computer Science and Artificial Intelligence Laboratory. 'Appropriate Reliance in Human-AI Systems.' *ACM Transactions on Interactive Intelligent Systems*, Vol. 14, No. 2

(2024). Teaching humans when to trust machines, which is apparently more complicated than teaching machines to be trustworthy.

University of California, Riverside. 'Water Usage in Large Language Model Training: Environmental Impact Assessment.' *Environmental Research Letters*, Vol. 19, 034029 (2024). Calculating that AI drinks water like a marathon runner in the desert, except the marathon never ends.

GOVERNMENT AND INTERNATIONAL ORGANISATION SOURCES

Commission for Regulation of Utilities, Ireland. 'Data Centre Impact on National Electricity System.' CRU/24/034, 2024. Ireland is discovering that hosting the world's cat videos requires more electricity than expected.

e-Governance Academy, Estonia. 'Digital Government Index 2024: Estonia Country Report.' Ministry of Economic Affairs and Communications, 2024. Estonia's digital success story proves that competent government is possible in countries small enough to fit in a spreadsheet.

European Parliament. 'Artificial Intelligence Act: Employment and Labour Relations Implications.' PE 734.004, 2024. The EU regulating AI with the speed of a glacier and the precision of a bureaucracy.

Iceland National Energy Authority. 'Data Centre Energy Consumption: Impact on National Grid.' Ministry of Industries and Innovation, 2024. Iceland is learning that infinite renewable energy meets its match in humanity's infinite appetite for computation.

Madrid City Council. 'Decide Madrid: Digital Participation Platform Impact Assessment.' Department of Citizen Participation, 2024. Spanish democracy embracing digital participation with Mediterranean passion and algorithmic precision.

Ministry of Education and Culture, Finland. 'Collaborative Intelligence Education: National Implementation Study.' *Finnish Education Research Journal*, Vol. 45, No. 2 (2024). Finland continues to make everyone else's education systems look inadequate, now with added AI.

Taiwan Digital Ministry. 'vTaiwan: Digital Democracy Platform Five-Year Impact Study.' Government of Taiwan Research Publications, 2024. Taiwan is proving that democracy and technology can coexist, assuming you have both technical competence and political will.

NOTE ON SOURCES

This bibliography represents a selection of key sources that informed the analysis in this volume. The rapid pace of AI development means that some citations may already be outdated by the time of publication – such is the nature of writing about a field that evolves faster than publishing cycles. All efforts have been made to verify facts and figures, though in a domain where 'facts' can become 'historical curiosities' overnight, a certain humility about accuracy is warranted.

The author acknowledges that any errors, misinterpretations, or outdated information remain entirely his responsibility. However, he reserves the right to blame them on hallucinating AI assistants if that makes everyone feel better about our algorithmic future.

Second edition sources

Liu, X. et al. (2019). 'A comparison of deep learning performance against health-care professionals in detecting disease from medical imaging.' *The Lancet Digital Health*, 1(6).

Li, P. et al. (2023). 'Making AI Less Thirsty.' arXiv:2304.03271 (subsequently published in *Communications of the ACM*). Provides GPT-3 water and energy consumption figures.

McDonald, G. (2024). *You Have Not Yet Heard Your Favorite Song: How Streaming Changes Music*. Kingston upon Thames: Canbury Press.

Central Statistics Office, Ireland (2024). Data-centre electricity consumption statistics (21% of national consumption for 2023).

UK House of Commons Library (2025). 'AI in UK Government Departments.' Research Briefing CBP-10236.

Katzenmeier, C. (2021). Medical liability and digital health under German law (legal framework reference for the disclosed composite liability scenario in Chapter 5).

ABOUT THE AUTHOR

Gari Johnson has spent over four decades observing the sales methodology revolution from the inside – first as a nineteen-year-old managing a door-to-door artwork sales team in 1980s Australia, and later as a senior executive at enterprise software leaders, including IBM, Oracle, Salesforce, Zendesk, and Alteryx, across the Asia Pacific markets.

This journey from street-level hustle to C-suite strategy gave Johnson a unique perspective on how selling evolved from intuitive relationship-building to formalised business science. His early management experience with direct sales operations taught him that "every no gets you closer to yes". It revealed the power of authentic storytelling – practical foundations that later informed his analysis of sophisticated enterprise methodologies.

Johnson's executive career included front-row seats to defining moments in the evolution of sales: the CRM wars between Siebel and Salesforce, Oracle's aggressive competitive strategies, the emergence of subscription-economy customer-success approaches, and the recent integration of AI-powered conversational intelligence into enterprise sales processes. At Alteryx, he led significant revenue growth in the APJ region. At Zendesk, his team closed the region's largest-ever transaction. At Salesforce, he built the Service Cloud business into the largest cloud unit in APAC.

As both practitioner and observer, Johnson implemented dozens of sales methodologies across diverse cultural contexts, from Australia's direct business culture to Japan's consensus-building approaches to Singapore's relationship-focused markets. This international experience revealed both universal principles of effective selling and the cultural adaptations required for successful global methodology.

Johnson's writing combines rigorous research with irreverent humour, reflecting his belief that the best insights emerge when we can laugh at our professional pretensions while maintaining respect for genuine innovation. His analysis benefits from insider knowledge of how methodology companies operate and from an outsider perspective on their claims of effectiveness.

Currently based in Sydney's Northern Beaches, Johnson continues to advise technology companies on balancing structured approaches with authentic customer relationships. He serves as a Winning By Design Ambassador and Executive Member of Pavilion, contributing to the evolution of modern revenue operations and go-to-market strategy.

Johnson holds certifications in multiple sales methodologies, language qualifications in Japanese and Mandarin, and decades of experience working through both professional success and personal challenges – including financial difficulties, family tragedies, and health crises that taught him resilience extends far beyond quarterly quotas.

When not deconstructing the industrial complex's methodology, Johnson plays guitar, cooks elaborate meals, and travels extensively to understand cross-cultural business relationships. He remains partnered with "the most incredible woman" and is the father of two exceptional children, whose growing families provide ongoing education in negotiation and maintaining perspective.

ABOUT THE SERIES

The Algorithmic Mind is a three-book series examining the social consequences of artificial intelligence. The series began from a straightforward observation: AI systems are not neutral tools. They reflect the priorities, histories, and blind spots of the people who built them and the societies from which their training data was drawn.

Book 1 – The Mirror Problem: How AI Reflects Our Worst Selves traces the sources of AI bias across race, gender, language, culture, and geography, and examines the governance frameworks being developed to address it.

Book 2 – The Surveillance Mirror: How Technology Watches You examines how AI systems that learn from human data generate new data about human behaviour – and how commercial and governmental actors use that data to influence the choices people make.

Book 3 – The Human Interface: Keeping People at the Centre turns to the question of how AI systems can be designed and governed so that the humans they affect remain genuinely in control of consequential decisions about their own lives.

The three books can be read independently. They form a coherent argument when read in sequence: first, what AI reflects; then, what AI watches; finally, what AI shapes.

www.ingramcontent.com/pod-product-compliance
Lightning Source LLC
LaVergne TN
LVHW022044200926
848481LV00003B/786